Field Day Survival Guide

Edited by Krista Winn

The Great Activities Publishing Company
PO Box 51158
Durham, North Carolina 27717

1 (800) 927-0682
www.greatactivities.net

Another great physical education publication
from the
Great Activities Publishing Company
PO Box 51158
Durham, North Carolina
27717-1158

Call 1 (800) 927-0682 for a free catalog!
www.greatactivities.net

ISBN: 0-945872-15-1

Cover design: Wendy Jackson

Table of Contents

Special Resources:

Certificate of Participation   32

Sportsmanship Award   40

Fit 4 Fun Certificate   92

Certificate of Honor   134

Teamwork Award   216

A+ for Effort Award   224

Certificate of
Achievement Award   229

Certificate of Merit   230

Best Partner Award   240

Activity Planning Sheet   248

Field Day Wall of Fame
Certificate   249

Super Parent
Volunteer Award   250

Friend of Physical
Education Award   251

Acknowledgements   2

Introduction   3

T.E.A.M. Field Day (K-2)   5

Day at the Races Field Day (PreK-5)   11

An Ocean of Fun Field Day (PreK-5)   19

County Fair Field Day (K-5)   25

Fun for All Field Day (K-3)   33

American Plains Field Day (K-5)   41

Great Relay Field Day (1-6)   49

Color Team Field Day (K-6)   55

Super Kids Field Day (K-5)   63

Fitness Festival Field Day (K-5)   75

School Pride Field Day (K-5)   93

Great Games Field Day (K-5)   99

World Records Field Day (K-5)   109

Think Tank Field Day (K-5)   117

International Games Field Day (K-5)   135

BINGO Field Day (K-5)   149

Fit, Healthy, and
Ready to Learn Field Day (K-5)   159

Livin' in the Country Field Day (K-5)   169

Olympics Field Day (K-5)   181

Teamwork Field Day (K-5)   199

Circle of Games Field Day (3-5)   217

Battle Creek Field Day Stations (K-5)   225

Wacky Olympics Field Day (K-5)   231

Field Day Sparklers (1-4)   241

Contributors   252

Acknowledgements

This project couldn't have been completed without the help of many people. I would like to warmly acknowledge the following individuals:

The Contributors - There were many physical educators who contributed to this book. The field day ideas, activities, and suggestions came from a wide-range of talented professionals across the nation. Their frequent e-mails of support and encouragement kept this project going. Their names are listed at the back of this book. Thanks!

Kristi Peck - Kristi, a fellow educator, volunteered to help with the original manuscript. Her word processing skills were a lifesaver!

Family - Tim Winn and our two great kids - Nels and Kelly - for their support during the entire project. They have been by my side through thick and thin: deadlines, computer crashes, and messy tables!

Campers and Counselors at Camp Hudson - Camp Hudson, in Gold Bar, Washington, served as a "training ground" for all of my crazy field day activities. We had root beer guzzling (including a dainty burp), dog bone searches, and spaghetti noodle hairdos. Luckily, none of these events made it into this project! But you have to start somewhere.

Students and Staff at Hamilton and Monroe Elementary Schools - It is my privilege to teach at Hamilton and Monroe Elementary Schools in Port Angeles, Washington. The field days at these schools are so successful because the entire school "family" is so involved. They are always prepared for the unexpected and are ready to participate with excitement and enthusiasm.

Special thanks to **Judy Brune**, for helping out all of these years. As a music education teacher, Judy was my colleague in planning many of our field days. We wish her a well-deserved retirement!

The Subscribers of Sportime's "P.E. Talk" - Last, but not least, I would like to thank Sportime's internet listserv that allows physical education professionals from around the world to share their ideas. It was our springtime field day conversations on "P.E. Talk" that sparked the interest in publishing this book!

Krista Winn
Port Angeles, Washington

Introduction

*** treasure chest *** croquet *** recycle relay ***

Field Day is a special year-end day of activities at many elementary schools across our nation. Field days have many variations:

- They can last all day or half day.
- Students can participate in classroom groups, mixed teams, or partner/individual "carnival-style" formats.
- Students can compete for prizes (competitive) or personal satisfaction (non-competitive).
- Some field days have a special theme or no theme at all.

No matter what the style or format, successful field days take quite a bit of time and energy to organize.

*** couch potato race *** slug on a stick ***

At our school, we create a new theme and choose appropriate activities so that no two years are alike. Personally, I get my best ideas while taking a shower. Well, after 14 years, there isn't much hot water left! But, with the help of Sportime's internet listserv, "P.E. Talk," I have been able to share ideas with other physical education teachers worldwide. "Anyone have any ideas for a water field day?" "I need help with a track and field day!" "I am looking for new activity ideas!" Veteran teachers and first-year teachers alike are constantly looking for help with organizing and implementing this annual event.

*** super soakers *** giant shoes *** towel toss ***

Throughout these on-line discussions, many physical education teachers and recreation program leaders have mentioned the need for a general book of ready-made field day ideas. Just think what a valuable resource a book of this type could be! At the very least, it could help us decrease our utility bills on hot water showers.

*** potato masher *** hay jump *** shuttle run ***

So this book, <u>Field Day Survival Guide</u>, is a collection of successful field day themes, activities, and helpful hints submitted by dedicated physical educators nationwide. The book is organized by contributors and the field days are presented as a whole from start to finish. Now you can implement a new field day without having to piece it together from different resources.

*** marble madness *** blob tag *** stork stand ***

Many of the contributors have included samples of memos, schedules, and awards. It is always difficult and time consuming to put letters together. The memo examples can aid all of us in writing our own memos to staff members, parents, and volunteers. Reproducible pages of sample book-marks, certificates, and other field day graphics are ready to use. These pre-made field days will save valuable time and energy.

*** chicken-catchatori *** crazy frog *** scooters ***

As mentioned before, our school's field days use a "carnival style" format with the students participating individually (or with partners) in games at their own pace. Other field day examples use activities where small groups of students move from station to station.

*** tootsie rolls *** synchronized sponges ***

The <u>Field Day Survival Guide</u> is a wonderful example of our professional teamwork. We saw a need for a field day resource and pooled our ideas to accomplish the task of making one. The ideas in this book are endless! I don't know which field day to start with!!

T.E.A.M. Field Day:

"Together Everyone Achieves More!"

T.E.A.M. - Together Everyone Achieves More!

Background: The "T.E.A.M. Field Day" was developed to encourage cooperation skills for K-2 students. At our school, we generally have up to 16 classes of K-2 students each year. With these large numbers, we have designed a morning and an afternoon field day. Half of the K-2 classes participate in the morning and the rest of the K-2 classes participate in the afternoon. While this format was designed with primary students in mind, please feel free to modify the activities to make the stations more successful and enjoyable for your older students. Parent volunteers and a 5th grade student helped to supervise each station. As you read the following station descriptions, please note that **each class is divided into four groups and rotates every 15 minutes to a new station**.

1. **The Raging River Crossing**

   Equipment: • 8 scooters
   • 4 thirty-foot ropes
   • 8 deck rings

   Description of the Activity: Use a basketball court for this station. One by one, each of the four groups will cross the "river" using the equipment (scooters, ropes, deck rings). All of the area between the shores (sideline to sideline) is considered water. The task is mastered when all of the team members have successfully crossed without touching the water. The equipment must also cross the river as well. If anyone touches the river, the group must go back and begin again.

2. **The Bridge Over Troubled Water**

   Equipment: • 4 flat balls
   • 4 big carpet squares and 4 little carpet squares
   • 4 poly spots
   • 4 cones
   • 4 bases

Procedures for Classroom Teachers

1. Divide your class into four groups. If possible, have an even number of students in each group. Each group will participate as a cooperative team at our activity stations.
2. Please stress "Teamwork and Cooperation!" We want everyone to have an active role in helping his or her team to be successful.
3. Your class will be at a station for 15 minutes. I will use the portable PA system to indicate when to rotate to the next station. Please rotate in sequential order - 1 goes to 2, 2 goes to 3, ... and 8 goes to 1.
4. You are responsible for discipline and bathroom passes throughout the T.E.A.M. Field Day.
5. 5th Grade Teachers: Please allow our student helpers to go to their stations at least 10 minutes early.
6. We have a designated "Time-Out" area for "disrupters." The parent volunteer at the "Time-Out" area will return the student to your class when you rotate to your next station. Please feel free to use this option as necessary.
7. There will be permanent station supervisors (parent volunteers) to manage each station with a 5th grade student helper.

Tentative Day's Schedule:

9:30 - 11:45   **Morning Field Day**: Designated K-2 classes are on the field and assigned to a beginning station.

11:55 - 12:20   Lunch

12:45 - 3:00   **Afternoon Field Day**: The rest of the K-2 classes are on the field.

3:00 - 3:15   PTSA classroom treats for all K-2 students.

Description of the Activity: This activity is similar to the "Raging River Crossing" station. Each of the four groups must use the available equipment to create a "moving bridge" to cross the river. The task is mastered when all team members have crossed the river with all equipment ashore. If anyone touches the river (the ground) with any body part, <u>all</u> of the students must start over.

3. **The Mine Field**

   Equipment:
   - Blindfolds
   - Hula hoops
   - Poly spots
   - Little cones, ropes, tennis balls, etc.

   Description of the Activity: The "mine field" consists of the available equipment spread out across the playing area. Have the students divide into pairs. One partner will be blindfolded. The other partner's job is to "talk" the blindfolded person across the field without touching one of the mines. Partners must start over if either of them touch a mine. Once across, the partners switch roles. If the first partner has not made it across after 5 minutes, have them switch roles.

   Send a few groups at a time. Let the first group get a few feet ahead before sending the next group. If partners have to start over, have them step to the side so they won't be in the way of other students behind them.

4. **The Creative Snake**

   Equipment: • 4 thirty-foot ropes

   Description of the Activity: The Creative Snake is a shape-building challenge using a rope to create the desired shapes. The teacher announces what shape to make with the rope. It should be a letter, number, shape, or object. After the team creates the desired shape, they must cover the rope completely by lying over it with their bodies. All of the team members must be part of the shape created. Each shape will be considered completed when approved by the teacher.

5.   **The Four Corners**

    Equipment: • 4 balance beams (or benches)
                          • Mats to cover the floor or ground

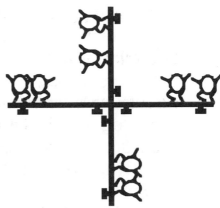

Description of the Activity: The "Four Corners" are created by making a "+" sign with four low balance beams or benches. Each team is issued the challenge to cooperate so that all of the team members touch each corner without stepping off the balance beams.

There is a 3-minute time limit to complete the mission, which makes this a very difficult task. Cooperation and communication are a must. The rest of the teams waiting for a turn should be watching and discussing how they can successfully complete this activity.

6.   **The Great Planet Pass**

    Equipment: • 2 cage balls
                          • 4 tires

Description of the Activity: The goal is to transfer the cage ball from one tire to the other (30 feet apart) without it touching the ground. Students cannot use their hands during this task. The task is successful when the cage ball is resting on the other tire. Two teams are attempting this while the other two are watching. Each team must try doing it in different ways. No copying another team!

Hints: You may allow the kindergarten and 1st grade students to use their hands, or allow the first teams up to use their hands. Possible solutions include: using their backs to hold the ball, using their heads, or using their bodies as railroad tracks while some students push the ball with body parts other than their hands.

7.   The Non-Stop Hoop Pass

Equipment: • 40 hula hoops

Description of the Activity:
This activity is performed by all four teams as a relay race. Each team must hold hands in a straight line and cannot let go. A pile of 10 hula hoops is placed at the feet of the first players in each line. On the teacher's signal, the first person in line will slip a hula hoop on his arm, get it over his head, step in it with one leg, step out of it with the other leg, and jiggle the hoop to the arm of the adjoining player. The task is to pass all 10 hula hoops through the line as quickly as possible. The relay is completed when all 10 hoops make it to the other end of the line. The first person may send another hoop as soon as the previous hoop touches the ground on the other side. If time per-, mits, try passing the hoops in the opposite direction.

8.   Traveling Heavy

Equipment: • 6-8 sponge balls
                         • 4 big cones

Description of the Activity:
The team's task is to travel to-gether from the starting line to the finish line (30 to 40 feet away) while holding a sponge ball between the shoulders of team members. If a ball drops, the team must start over.

This is not a race. Also have them try this with the balls between their hips, then their legs.

Day at the Races Field Day:

A Multi-Aged Field Day Format

"Day at the Races" Field Day

Background: This field day uses a **multi-age (PreK - 5th Grade) group format** and consists of 11 activity stations, a rest station, and a snack station. Unless otherwise noted, all of the activities are done **with 3-4 teams in a single-file relay formation**. Led by a teacher or teacher assistant, each group rotates through the stations at **10-minute** intervals. All of the stations are directed by parent volunteers who divide the students into teams once they arrive at a station. In this way, the students are on different teams each time they go to a new activity.

1. **America's Cup Sailing Race**

   Equipment:
   - 2 non-steel belted car tires cut in half (like you'd slice a bagel)
   - 4 ping pong balls
   - Water

Filled with water

 Description of the Activity: On the signal to start, the first person on each team runs to the tire, which is filled with water, and begins "sailing" his vessel (ping pong ball) around the tire by blowing on it. After completing a lap, this player returns to the starting line and the next person repeats the same activity.

2. **The Fort Wayne 500**

   Equipment:
   - 4 auto tires
   - 4 cones

Description of the Activity: On the signal to start, the racers begin hand rolling their tires around a designated course. When a racer completes a lap, he hands the tire off to the next player who repeats the same activity.

Regarding Multi-Age Group Field Days

Each year we select a theme for our school's field day activities. These activities are easy to do, silly, and strictly for fun. Finishing first is not as important as having a good time.

The teacher responsibilities include helping to organize students at each station, chaperoning their groups from station to station, and helping the parent volunteers.

Unlike some field days, which last the entire day, ours is about 2 to 2-1/2 hours long. If possible, we try to provide a treat for the kids, either as a station or after our field day is over.

In the past, we did not award ribbons of any kind. However, we now purchase participation ribbons depicting the theme of the field day. Our school's PTA provides the ribbons, refreshments for the parent volunteers and students, and miscellaneous supplies.

I have also included a sample master schedule and a sample letter to our parent volunteers. Special thanks to the teachers at the Diocese of Fort Wayne-South Bend, the contributors to the Great Activities Newspaper and Sportime's "PE-Talk" (www.sportime.com/pe-talk).

3. **The International Funny Car Races**

    Equipment: • 4 cardboard "cars" (large cardboard box)
    • 4 cones

    Description of the Activity: On the signal to start, the first person on each team gets into the "car," holds the car with their hands, and begins running to the cone and back. This driver exits the car and the next driver gets in to continue the relay.

4. **The Wateree River Raft Race**

    Equipment: • 4 scooter boards
    • 4 "oars" (hockey stick or homemade oar)
    • 4 cones
    • Several super soaker water guns
    • Water supply

    Description of the Activity: On the signal to start, the first person on each team begins riding the raft (scooter board) - seated or kneeling - using his feet or hands to move himself to the cone and back. They must do this while keeping the "oar" in their possession at all times; after all, they cannot go up the river without the paddle! Upon returning, the first rider gets off and the second rider gets on and repeats the relay. The super soakers are for the volunteer parents directing the activity. They can soak the rafters as they navigate the course!

5. **The Hospital Bed Race**

    Equipment: • 4 folding mats
    • 16 scooter boards
    • 4 carpet squares (pillows)
    • 4 cones

    Description of the Activity: Place a mat on top of several scooter boards and use a carpet square as a pillow. The first person in line will lie down on the "bed." The second person in line pushes the bed to the turn-around point, where the rider and the pusher change places before returning. The next two students repeat the same activity.

6. **The Pit Stop**: This is the restroom/drink station.

7. **The Original Open Field Foot Race**

Equipment:
- 4 batons
- 4 cones

Description of the Activity: On the signal to start, the first player on each team runs to a turn-around point and back again, where he hands the baton to the second runner. This continues until a designated number of runs have been completed.

8. **The Tour de Foot**

Equipment:
- 4 tricycles
- 4 cones

Description of the Activity: On the signal to start, the first racer on each team rides around the cone and back. If a rider cannot pedal, he should propel the trike "Flintstone" style. The first rider then gets off the trike and hands it to the next person who repeats the same activity.

9. **Rodeo Barrel Racing**

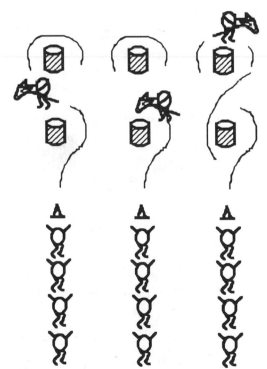

Equipment:
- 4 stick horses
- 8 plastic trash cans or cones ("barrels")
- 4 cones

Description of the Activity: Place two barrels in front of each team, with the first about 15 feet away and the second about 30 feet away.

On the signal to begin, team members take turns riding their horse, weaving in and out of the two barrels.

10. The Drag Races

Equipment:
- 4 sandbags with rope attached
- 4 cones

Description of the Activity: The students take turns dragging their sandbag around the cone and back.

11. The "Fill it Up" Relay

Equipment:
- 4 2-liter soda bottles
- 4 sponges
- 4 buckets of water

Description of the Activity: On the signal to begin, the first person in each line dips the sponge in the bucket of water, which is at the front of the line. He begins passing the sponge down the line until it reaches the last person, who squeezes the water into the bottle. This person then returns to the bucket to soak the sponge before handing it down the line again. The first team to fill the bottle to a designated level is the winner.

12. Santa Fe Hot Air Balloon Races

Equipment:
- 4 chairs per team
- 1 balloon per student

Description of the Activity: The students carry a balloon to a chair where they attempt to pop it by sitting on it. Once the balloon has popped, the student returns to his line and the next person repeats the same activity.

13. The Derby Day Concession Stand: This is the snack station.

Sample Master Schedule

Background Information to Teachers: Listed below is the master schedule for our field day. As you know, you have been asked to divide the students in your class into **13 groups**. For the typical class of 26 students, this will mean two students per group. The field day consists of 13 different stations. We will gather together on the outdoor basketball court.

Once the general field day directions have been given, please direct your students to go to their designated stations. Students in Group #1 will go to Station #1, students in Group #2 will go to Station #2, etc. Each station is clearly marked with a huge sign with the number written on it. Just in case, I will point out each station to the students before they are dismissed from the basketball court. Thanks!

Time:	Activity:
9:00 AM:	All gather at the outdoor basketball court for directions.
9:15 AM	Students go to their respective stations #1-#13.
9:20 AM	First station begins **(I'll use the PA system to start and stop).**
9:30 AM	First station ends, move to the next station.
9:40 AM	Second station ends, move to the next station.
9:50 AM	Third station ends, move to the next station.
10:00 AM	Fourth station ends, move to the next station.
10:10 AM	Fifth station ends, move to the next station.
10:20 AM	Sixth station ends, move to the next station.
10:30 AM	Seventh station ends, move to the next station.
10:40 AM	Eighth station ends, move to the next station.
10:50 AM	Ninth station ends, move to the next station.
11:00 AM	Tenth station ends, move to the next station.
11:10 AM	Eleventh station ends, move to the next station.
11:20 AM	Twelfth station ends, move to the next station.
11:30 AM	Last station ends, all report back to the basketball court. and line up as directed by your teacher.
11:40 AM	Dismissed to "Lunch on the Lawn."

Have a Great Field Day!

"Day at the Races" Field Day

Sample Letter to Parents

Field Day is Coming!	We need your help to make our field day a success! Like last year's event, we need about 2-3 parent volunteers per class to help direct our 13 field day stations.

Great, New Look!	This year's field day is called "A Day at the Races." It is a multi-aged field day with a wide variety of neat games and activities. Listen to some of the fun stations we will have this year -

- "America's Cup Sailing Races"
- "The International Funny Car Races"
- "The Hospital Bed Race"
- "Rodeo Barrel Racing"
- "The Tour de Foot," and more!

Please Help Us!	I have asked each classroom teacher to find 2-3 parent volunteers to help at our field day stations. Please fill out and return the form below if you can help this year. As always, we appreciate your involvement in making this the best field day ever! If you have any questions, please contact me at _____.

Volunteer Form

Please return this to your child's classroom teacher by May 1st.

Thank you!

Yes!, I would love to help at the "Day at the Races" Field Day, May 23rd from 8:30 AM - 12:00 noon. Rain date is May 30th. Lunch will be provide for all parent volunteers!

My Name: _____
Home Phone: _____
Work Phone: _____
Classroom Teacher: _____

18

An Ocean of Fun Field Day:

Another Multi-Aged Field Day Format

"An Ocean of Fun" Field Day

Background: Many of the station ideas in this field day are from the "Field Day Queen," Judy Rawlins of Appling, Georgia. Her field day ideas have appeared in past issues of The Great Activities Newspaper. This is a modification of Judy's "20,000 Leagues Under the Sea" Field Day.

Like the "Day at the Races" Field Day, **we use multi-aged (PreK-5) groups** of 26-30 players **(See page 17: Background Information to Teachers)**. Led by a teacher or teacher assistant, each group rotates through the stations at **10-minute intervals**. All of the stations are directed by parent volunteers who divide the students into teams when they arrive at a station.

In this way, the students are on different teams each time they move to a new activity. Each team should have several members from each of the participating grade levels. **Unless otherwise noted, all of the activities are arranged with 3-4 teams in a single-file relay formation**.

1. **The Giant Octopus Relay**

   Equipment:
   - 24-32 "cans of tuna" (pucks, balls, etc.)
   - 8 hoops
   - 4 ropes (tied to form a circle) or bicycle inner tubes

   Description of the Activity: Each team member grasps the rope or inner tube with one hand, leaving the outside hand (tentacle) free. On the signal to start, each octopus moves around the field, picking up one can of tuna at each of the eight sites (hoops). Each octopus may travel to the hoops in any order, but may pick up only one can of tuna at each site. The first octopus to collect eight cans of tuna and return to the starting line is the winner.

20

2.   The Snorkeling Adventure

> **Equipment:**   • 1 straw per student
> •   24-32 paper fish
> •   8 pails
> •   4 cones

Description of the Activity: On the signal to start, one player from each team runs forward to the pail containing fish. This player picks up a snorkeling tube (straw) and attempts to suck a fish from the pail, and transfer it to the other pail without touching the fish with his hands. After doing this, this player throws the straw away and returns to the line to tag the next player.

3.   Barracuda Boogie

> **Equipment:**   • 4 burlap bags
> •   8 cones

Description of the Activity: On the signal to start, the first person on each team steps into the sack and begins jumping toward the cone. Here he steps out of the sack and runs back with the sack to the line where the next person repeats the same activity.

4.   Underwater Treasures

> **Equipment:**   • 1 wading pool
> •   100 marbles
> •   4 buckets
> •   4 cones

Description of the Activity: Fill the wading pool with water and marbles. On the signal to start, the first player on each team runs to the pool, removes his shoes and uses his toes to pick up a marble which he drops in his team's bucket. This is then repeated by the remaining members of the team. The first team to have 20 marbles wins.

5.   The Submarine Races

Equipment: • 4 inflatable pool
               floats (or folding
               mats)
            • 8 cones

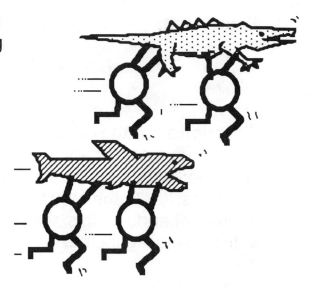

Description of the Activity: On
the signal to start, the first two
people on each team hold the
float/mat overhead and begin
running to the cone and back
again. This continues until each
team has completed the race a
designated number of times.

6.   The Ocean Rescue Relay

Equipment: • 4 lifesaver rings or vests (styrofoam or inflatable)

Description of the Activity: Position the teams in single-file lines
with one person from each team standing about 30 feet away facing
his team. On the signal to start, the person standing opposite the
team carries the lifesaver ring to the first person in line. This person is
"rescued" by holding on to the ring and being taken back to shore by
the rescuer. Upon reaching shore, the rescued person then becomes
the new rescuer and now rescues the next player in line.

7.   Hoist the Sails

Equipment: • Tug-of-war rope with a center flag
            • 2 cones

Description of the Activity: This is a tug-of-war activity. On the
signal, the two teams begin pulling. When one team has pulled the
rope far enough for the center flag to pass over a designated mark,
the sails have successfully been hoisted.

8.   The Beach House: This is the rest/restroom station.

9. **The Catch of the Day**

   Equipment:
   - 4 five-gallon buckets
   - 1-2 wading pools
   - Water balloons

   Description of the Activity: On the signal to begin, the first person in each line runs to the pool to get a fish (balloon). He tosses it to the next player who passes it to the next and so on. The last person in line places the "catch of the day" into the bucket. The first player runs back, tags the next player, and goes to the end of the line. The first team to place a designated number of fish in the bucket is the winner.

10. **The S.O.S. (Save Our Ship) Relay**

    Equipment:
    - 4 five-gallon buckets
    - 4 small barrels (or trash can)
    - 4 "leaky" cups

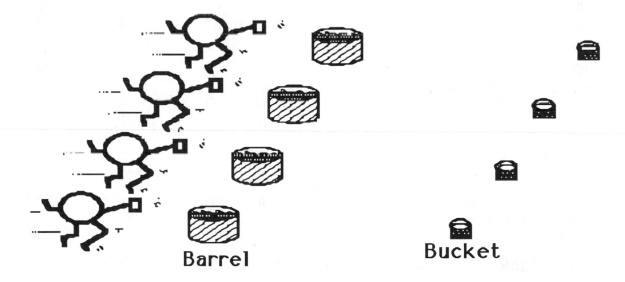

Barrel   Bucket

Description of the Activity: On the signal to start, the first person on each team carries his team's cup to the barrel that is filled with water. He fills his cup and then quickly runs to the bucket and dumps the water before returning to the line. The next person then repeats the same race. The first team to fill the bucket up to a designated line is the winner.

11. The SCUBA Scramble

Equipment:
- 4 sets of swim fins and goggles
- 4 swim rings
- 12 hoops
- 4 cones

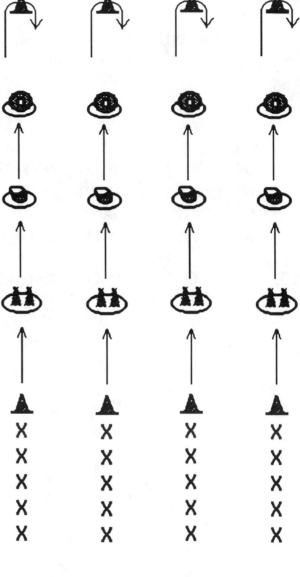

Description of the Activity:
On the signal to begin, the first person in each line runs forward to the first hoop where they put on the swim fins.

At the second hoop the players put on the swimming goggles. At the third hoop they place an inflatable swim ring around their waists. After putting on all of the items, the players continue to the cones at the end of the course, run around them, and return.

On the way back, the runners must remove the items in the reverse order and place them back in the hoops. Each player tags the next runner in line as the relay continues.

12. The Snack Hut: This is the snack and water station. It's time for a break!

Field Day Survival Guide

County Fair Field Day

"County Fair" Field Day

Background: The stations for this field day each have an old fashioned county fair theme. This field day format accommodates **up to seven classes at a time. Each class is divided into two smaller groups of 12-14 students**. Led by a teacher or a parent volunteer, each group is assigned to one of the **14 stations** to begin the field day. Unless otherwise designated, all of the activities are performed **in a relay formation**. Each station is managed by several parent volunteers.

```
┌─────────────────────────────┐
│                             │
│   Score Card                │
│   We started at             │
│   Station ☛ ____            │
│                             │
│   1. _____   8. _____    │
│   2. _____   9. _____    │
│   3. _____  10. _____    │
│   4. _____  11. _____    │
│   5. _____  12. _____    │
│   6. _____  13. _____    │
│   7. _____  14. _____    │
│                             │
└─────────────────────────────┘
```

The groups rotate through the stations at **10-minute intervals** as directed by the physical education teacher using a sound system set-up near the field day site. The physical education teacher will allow time for the parent volunteers to explain the activity, announce when it is time to start and end the activity, and give time to total the points before rotating to the next station. While at each station, the students earn points for their group. These points are recorded on the group's score card by the parent volunteer. Up to 10 bonus points can be given by the parent volunteers if the group listens carefully and is ready to rotate to the next station on time. Challenge the groups to score more than 1,000 points during the field day!

1.   **Driving the Pigs to Market**

      Equipment: • 2 hockey sticks
                    • 2 playground balls
                    • 2 cones

      Description of the Activity: On the signal to start, the first person begins using the stick to push the ball ("pig") to the cone and back. When this is done, 1 point is earned for the group. Remind the students that the stick is used to push, not hit, the ball. Students are not allowed to swing the hockey stick.

2.   Sack Race and Three Legged Race

Equipment: • 2 burlap sacks
                • 4 cones

Description of the Activity: On the signal to start, the first person in line steps into the sack and jumps to the cone. Once at the cone, the person steps out of the sack and runs back with the sack to his team. One point is earned when this happens. This continues for about 4 minutes.

After the sack races, run the three-legged race. Each student needs a partner. The partners stand side by side, placing one leg into the sack. Together they "run" to the cone and back. When this happens 2 points are scored. Continue until time is called. Remind the students that up to 10 bonus points can be given if the group listens carefully and is ready to rotate to the next station on time.

3.   The Soup Spoon Race

Equipment: • 2 wooden spoons
                • 2 plastic eggs
                • 4 cones

Description of the Activity: The first person should have a spoon and an egg. On the signal to start, this player runs to the cone and back while carrying the egg on the spoon. If the egg falls it must be picked up with the spoon, not the hand.

Two points are scored each time a student successfully completes the course. Award up to 10 bonus points for good student behavior.

4.   **Find the Needle in the Haystack**

   Equipment: • Colored toothpicks
                   • 2 small buckets or bags

   Description of the Activity: On the signal to start, the first person runs to the "haystack" (grassy area) and begins searching for needles (toothpicks), collecting as many as possible. The parent volunteer will give each player about 30 seconds. When time expires, he returns to the line and the next player resumes the search. Score 1 point for every toothpick collected. Award up to 10 bonus points for good student behavior.

5.   **Milking the Cow**

   Equipment: • 2 large buckets
                   • 2 small buckets
                   • 2 sponges

   Description of the Activity: On the signal to start, the first player runs to the large bucket which contains the "milk" (water). He dips the sponge into the water and carries it to the smaller bucket where the sponge is wrung out.

   The sponge is then given to the next player. The team earns 100 points each time the bucket is filled to the top (or to the designated level). When this happens, pour the water out of the small bucket and continue until time is up. Award up to 10 bonus points for good student behavior.

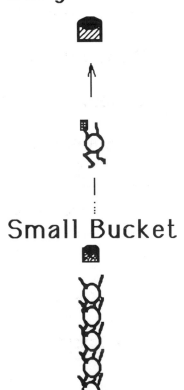

   Large Bucket

   Small Bucket

6.   **The Outhouse:** This is the restroom/drink station.

7. **The Firewood Fetch**

   Equipment: • 24-28 sticks of wood, about 1" in diameter

   Description of the Activity: Place 12-14 sticks in a small pile about 30 feet in front of each group. On the signal to start, the first player runs to the woodpile and picks up one piece of "firewood" before returning to the starting line where he hands the wood to the next player. The second player carries the first stick to the woodpile and adds a second stick. Both sticks are then carried back and given to the third person who retrieves a third stick and so on. The last person will have to carry all the sticks back from the pile. Score one point each time a player completes the course. As time permits, return the sticks to the woodpile and begin again. Award up to 10 bonus points for good student behavior.

8. **The Egg Toss**

   Equipment: • Water balloons ("eggs")

   Description of the Activity: Divide the students into partners. Partners stand about 5 feet apart from each other. On the signal to start, the partners begin tossing their balloon. If it doesn't break, they can continue to participate in the contest after taking one giant step backward. Award 10 points for each set of partners able to make it past three steps. Award bonus points for good student behavior.

9. **Bucket Run**

   Equipment:

   •   2 small buckets
   •   Water
   •   4 cones
   •   2 measuring sticks

**3" or more =
20 extra points**

Description of the Activity: On the signal to start, the first person will pick up the bucket of water and begin running to the cone and back. One point is earned when this happens. The bucket is handed to the next person in line who repeats the activity. This continues until time is up. The team with the most water remaining in its bucket is the winner.

10. **The Cross Country Pony Express**

Equipment:
- 2 stick ponies
- 2 backpacks
- 4 cones

Description of the Activity: On the signal to start, the first person begins riding the pony to the cone and back. The backpack and pony are then handed off to the next rider.

This continues until time is up. Score 1 point for each player. Award bonus points for good student behavior.

11. **The Bubble Blowing Contest**

Equipment:
- Bubble wands
- Bubble solution

Description of the Activity: This activity is just for fun. Students can scatter and spend a few minutes having fun making soap bubbles. Award up to 100 points for good student behavior.

12. **Rope Jumping Contest**

Equipment:
- 2 long jump ropes

Description of the Activity: The students take turns jumping rope. Two students are the turners. One by one, the students have a turn jumping the long rope. Each student earns 1 point for each consecutive jump completed without error. Total all of the points for the team score. Award bonus points for good student behavior.

13.   The Frog Jumping Contest

   Equipment: • 4 cones

   Description of the Activity: On the signal to start, the first two students begin leapfrogging (one stoops while the other leaps over) to the cone and back. Score 2 points each time the partners complete the course. This continues until time is up. Award bonus points for good student behavior.

14.   Country Vittles: This is the snack/treat station.

Certificate of Participation

Presented to: _____

What a Fun Field Day!

Great Activities Publishing Company

Fun for All Field Day

"Fun for All" Field Day

Background: Welcome to the "Fun for All" Field Day. Each year we design a field day **based on fun relays**. The number of relays we have is determined on how many classes we have, available space, time, etc.

Student Volunteers: For our field day, we do not use parent volunteers. Instead we use 4th and 5th grade student volunteers. The students do an excellent job of running the stations. Prior to field day, the student volunteers are videotaped doing the stations. We show this video to our classes the day before as a preview of what's to come.

Each student volunteer is in charge of a station for an assigned time. They are instructed to demonstrate the station, then make it fun for the classes. It is great to watch them encourage the kindergarten students and make an activity more challenging to the older students and their peers. Many of our student helpers decide to stay on and work an extra shift. We reward them by providing a drink and snack throughout the day. One year we had a private water balloon fight just for the helpers.

Set-Up and Clean-Up: We set up everything early in the morning. There are always **three lines** at every station. Allow **10-15 minutes for each station** (depending on the number of students participating). We use an equipment checklist prior to field day and pack everything in boxes the day before. At the end of the day, the volunteer student helpers bring in their equipment. The entire grounds are cleared in 5 minutes.

Day's Format: The students watch a video of last year's teachers' relay events and talent show, participate in the field day activities (including an art activity), have a class picnic, and watch the special teacher assembly:

- **Video in Room:** This is a video of last year's teachers competing in field events against other teachers.
- **Field Events:** Our outdoor stations of relays.
- **Art Activities:** Students participate in two of these activities.
- **Class Picnic:** Each class plans their own picnic.
- **The Teacher Assembly:** At the end of the day all of the students

gather in the gym to watch the teachers compete in relays. We use three teams of four teachers and they never know what they will be doing. We have a very talented staff member who is our "Master of Ceremonies." In addition to the teacher relays, we also have a staff talent contest. We videotape this and show it at next year's field day.

Talented Teachers: Examples of teacher entertainment includes teacher cheerleaders, skits, and our principal doing a double dutch routine. We use lots of music, props and sound effects during our Teacher Assembly.

My favorite Teacher Assembly was the year we did the "Teacher Olympics." Teachers participated in a basketball dribbling relay, a figure eight marathon around the gym, and an equestrian event by riding hockey sticks (with horse manes attached) and jumping over hurdles. The students look forward to this as much as the other activities.

"If You Had Fun, You Won!" We do not give prizes, awards, or keep score in any way. We encourage everyone to set their own goals and take pride in doing their best. Some of the classroom teachers give awards for sportsmanship or make Gold Medals for their students.

Schedule:

Day Before:	Show the video to each classroom of the student volunteers demonstrating each activity
Day of the Field Day:	
8:45 AM	Last year's video highlights shown in each classroom
9:00 AM	Classes assemble outside
9:10 AM - 11:30 AM	The "Fun for All" Field Day Stations
11:30 AM - 1:00 PM	Class picnics
1:00 PM - 2:00 PM	Teacher Assembly in the gym
2:00 PM	Students return to their classrooms

"Fun for All" Field Day Stations

1. **Disc Bowling Lanes**

   Equipment:
   - 9 foam discs
   - 3 plastic bowling pins

   Description of the Activity: Each line has three foam discs. The first person in each line throws the disc, frisbee style, to knock down the pin. Up to three chances are given each player. The thrower must then retrieve the discs and set up the pin for the next thrower. How many times can you knock down the pin?

2. **The Mouse Escape**

   Equipment:
   - 9 tennis balls
   - 3 cardboard boxes cut and painted to look like mouse holes

   Description of the Activity: Each line has three tennis balls. The first person in each line tries to help the mouse (tennis ball) get back into his hole by rolling the tennis ball through the mouse hole. How many mice can you get into the hole?

3. **The Four-legged Relay**

   Equipment:
   - 3 pairs of shoes
   - Cones

   Description of the Activity: The first person in each line places his hands in the shoes and runs on hands and feet around the cone and back. How many times can your group win the race?

4. **The Sock Toss**

   Equipment:

   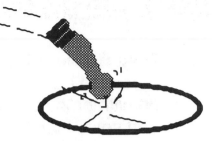

   • 9 socks with a
     tennis ball inside each sock (sock-tails)
   • 3 hula hoops

   Description of the Activity: The first person in each line picks up the sock by the tail. The challenge is to toss the sock so that it lands in the hoop. Students run to retrieve the sock for the next tosser. How many sock-tails can you get to land in the hoop?

5. **The Croquet Course**

   Equipment: • 3 hockey sticks
                  • 3 whiffle balls
                  • 9 wickets
                  • Cones

   Description of the Activity: The first person in line uses the hockey stick to move the ball through all three of the wickets and around the cone. The student goes straight back to the next person in line.

6. **The Funnel Ball Game**

   Equipment: • Funnel (playground equipment)
                  • 3 playground balls

   Description of the Activity: Each line faces the funnel (this is a piece of equipment on our playground). The first person in line tosses the ball into the funnel, retrieves the ball and then gives it to the next person. How many shots can you make?

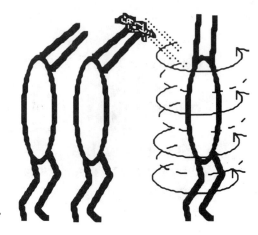

7. **The Chicken Rotisserie**

   Equipment: • 3 rubber chickens

   Description of the Activity: The first person in each line picks up the chicken with both hands, holds it overhead and spins in a circle. Immediately after spinning, the person passes the chicken overhead to the next person in line. This player spins and passes the chicken to the next player. When the chicken reaches the end of the line, that person runs to the front to begin the process again.

8. **The Recycling Relay**

   Equipment: • 3 boxes (recycle bins)
   • Assorted plastic and cardboard items
   • 6 hula hoops

   Description of the Activity: The first person in line picks up the box of assorted items and carries it to the hoops to sort the plastic into one hoop and the cardboard into the other hoop. When completed, he returns to the next runner with an empty box. The next runner must collect both plastic and cardboard from the hoops and return the full box to the next runner who repeats the pattern of the first runner.

9. **Carry All You Can**

   Equipment: • 9 balls
   • 3 hula hoops
   • 3 batons
   • 3 cones

   Description of the Activity: The first person in line carries all of the equipment down to the cone and back to the next runner who does the same. A suggested method of carrying is: a ball in each hand, hoop over a shoulder, baton under the chin, and dribble the remaining ball with the foot.

10. **The Matching Relay**

    Equipment: • Frisbees with numbers (1, 2, 3 or 4) written on the bottom

    Description of the Activity: The first person in each line runs to get a frisbee and runs back to his line. The next person runs to pick up another frisbee and runs back hoping to match the number on the first one. If the numbers match, the team keeps both frisbees and the third runner runs to get a new frisbee. If the first numbers do not match, the third runner must take back the second runner's frisbee and pick up a different one. Continue the procedure of keeping pairs that match and returning frisbees that don't. The runner must keep the frisbee he picks up even if he knows it is not a match. Helpers will need to spread out all of the frisbees, number side down, for the next group.

11. **The Plunger Ball Carry**

    Equipment: • 3 plungers
    • 3 nerf soccer balls
    • 3 cones

    Description of the Activity: The first person in line places the ball in the cup end of a plunger. Holding the stick of the plunger and keeping the cup end upright, the student runs to the cone and back without dropping the ball. Runners may not stuff the ball into the plunger.

12. **The Art Activities Station:** The students may select one of the following activities.

    • **Origami:** The students can fold the colored paper into a variety of different objects.
    • **Artist in the Dark:** Each student closes his eyes and draws as directed by an adult. Example: Draw a house, put a chimney on the house, add two windows, add smoke coming out the chimney, etc.
    • **Sidewalk Drawing:** Each student fills a square of the sidewalk with any type of chalk drawing he chooses. This is quite a work of art after all 600+ students have finished.

Sportsmanship Award

The Bearer of this Certificate has Displayed Outstanding Sportsmanship During Our Field Day

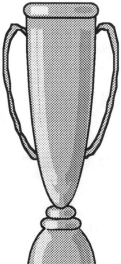

Physical Education Teacher

Principal

Great Activities Publishing Company

American Plains Field Day

"American Plains" Field Day

Background: This field day has been very popular in our school. Each of the 12 stations is supervised by a parent volunteer. The classroom teacher accompanies his or her class and assists the parent volunteer in helping to organize the students at each station. Each class is assigned a beginning station and rotates from station to station during the field day. In most instances, the students are divided into **four groups** (tribes) and **participate relay-style**.

Field Day Beads: Each of the students is given a piece of lanyard or colorful cord. As the students complete each station, the parent volunteer gives each student a colored bead. Each of the 12 stations has a different colored bead. The students tie a knot between each bead so that they will stay in place on the cord.

At the end of the field day, each student has created a 12-bead necklace. This is their own necklace to remember their field day activities. The beads and plastic lanyard are purchased at a local craft store. The PTA covers the cost of the 12 beads and 1 yard of lanyard per student.

Field Day Format: Our kindergarten to second grade classes start at 9:00 am and finish at 11:00 am. This allows the kindergarten students to eat at their regular time. Additional parent volunteers and the classroom teachers rotate with the students from station to station. The extra parents can also help with tying the beads on the lanyard or cord.

Upper Grades: These classes participate from 12:45 pm - 2:45 pm. Each group starts at a different numbered station and proceeds through the 12 events in sequence. Once again, there are parent volunteers who manage each station. Groups spend approximately **10 minutes** at each event. The teachers rotate at their own pace and are able to get to all 12 stations in this time period.

Refreshments: Refreshments are at a separate station. Teachers can direct their students to the refreshment station as needed. This time is also used as a restroom and water break.

1.   **The Raging Rapids River Race**

Equipment: • 4 sponges
                 • 1 small wading pool
                 • 4 buckets

Description of the Activity: On the signal to begin, the first person in each line takes the sponge and runs to the river (wading pool). The player soaks the sponge and returns to his team where he wrings the water from the sponge into the tribe's water supply (bucket). Continue until each tribe has filled the bucket to the top. Repeat as time permits.

2.   **The Painted Pony Race**

Equipment: • 4 scooters
                 • 4 cones

Description of the Activity: The scooters are used as the ponies. The first students in each line sit on the scooter backwards and use their feet to push themselves to the cone and back. For safety reasons, please tell the students to keep their hands from under the scooters. The first tribe to complete 25 laps is declared the winner.

3.   **The Toss Ball Game**

Equipment:

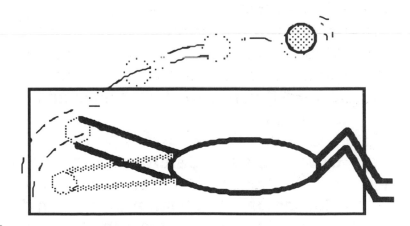

• Volleyballs, large foamballs, or playground balls
• Mats

Description of the Activity: While lying on their backs, arms outstretched overhead, the students try to heave the ball as far as they can without lifting their bodies off of the ground. Who will throw the ball the greatest distance? Play several rounds as time permits.

4. The Pine Cone Toss

Equipment:
- Pine cones
- One hanging hula hoop per group (hang the hoop from a soccer goal or from a set of volleyball standards with a rope stretched between them)

Description of the Activity: The students try to toss the four pine cones through the hoops. Set up as many groups as space allows.

5. The Kickball Race

Equipment:
- 8 cones
- 2 soccer balls

Description of the Activity: Divide the class in half. Cones are set up so that the students dribble figure-8 style around the four cones and back. Vary the distance between cones depending on the ages of the students. The first group to complete 20 circuits is the winner.

6. Lance Throw

Equipment:
- 4 pool fun noodles

Description of the Activity:
This activity is done in relay formation. Divide the class into four groups. Starting at the designated line, the first four students toss the "lance" (fun noodle) for distance and then retrieve it for the next person in line.

7. Bowl Toss and Catch

Equipment:
- 6 foam circles with designs on one side (paper plates with student-made designs also work well)
- Large plastic mixing bowl

Description of the Activity: Put the six foam circles in the bowl. One player flips the circles by tossing the bowl up (do not let go!) and catching them back in the bowl. Add up the score as shown below. Let the next person play.

Scoring:

If a circle lands design up = 1 point

If a circle lands blank side up = 0 points

Circles that land outside of the bowl = 0 points

---

8. **The River Jump**

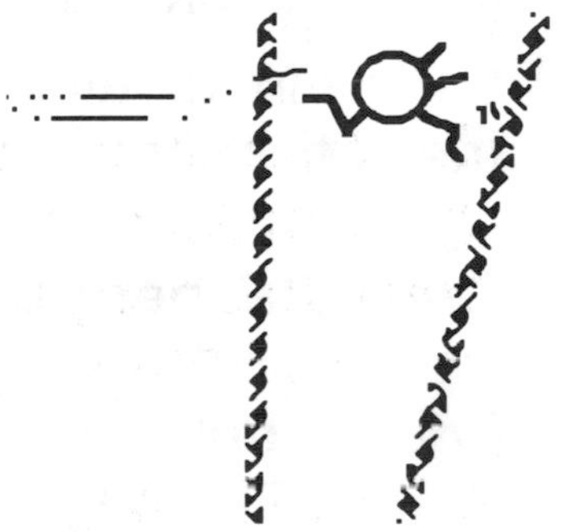

Equipment: • 2 long jump ropes

Description of the Activity: This activity is done like the long jump. The students are in one long line. Place two jump ropes on the ground approximately 2 feet apart. Students take a short run, taking off of one foot and jumping over the distance landing on two feet with knees bent. The rope is moved wider after everyone has had a turn. The ropes should be somewhat "v" shaped to allow your students to jump across the wide or narrow portion as they choose.

9. **The Fishing Hole**

Equipment: • Wading pool
  • Marbles
  • 4 frisbees

Description of the Activity: Students take off one shoe and one sock. On the signal to begin, the first student in each line hops to the pool and dips the uncovered foot in the pool, picking up one marble with his toes. He then places the marble in his team's frisbee and hops back to the line to tag the next person. The first team to get 10 marbles is the winner.

10. The Corn Cob Foot Toss

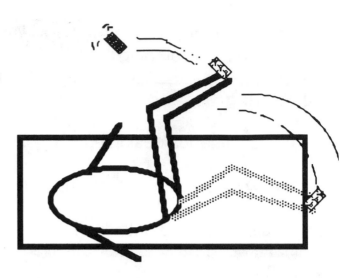

Equipment: • 8 corn cobs
• Mats

Description of the Activity:
Divide the class into four groups. Each group is given two corn cobs. The students lie down on their backs with their heads at the starting line. Placing a corn cob between the arches of the feet, the students toss the corn cob by lifting their legs quickly over their heads and letting go of the corn cob so it travels in the air for distance. Students get two chances, then retrieve the corn cobs for the next player.

11. Crazy Badger Run

Equipment: • Variety of equipment to make an obstacle course (it varies on the amount and type of equipment your school may have)

Description of the Activity: The students go through the obstacle course and then run beside the course on the return to tag the next person in line. Divide the class into lines based on how many courses you can set up.

12. Water Stand Up

Equipment: • 4 plastic or paper cups
• Water

Description of the Activity: The first students in each line lie down on their backs. The volunteer places a cup of water on each of the the four students' foreheads. The students try to stand up without tipping or spilling the cup of water. If successful at getting up, they can try going back down to their original lying position.

Extra Stations

Listed below are five extra stations that our older students enjoy. These can be used to supplement or substitute for the original 12 stations.

13. The Stick Pull

Equipment:
- One stick per pair (old broom handles work well)
- Mats

Description of the Activity: The students sit facing each other with the bottoms of their feet together. Both students grip the stick with two hands. One person will have the inside hand grip, and the other person will have the outside hand grip. Both students pull on the stick, trying to either pull it out of their partner's hand or to lift their partner up out of his starting position. Make sure that the students do not let go of the stick too early and that they do not land on other students.

14. One Foot High Kick

Equipment:
- Sock balls - tied with a rope to a folding chair
- Basketball hoop (to hang sock from)

Description of the Activity: Hang the sock/yarn ball from the basketball hoop. The rope should go through the hoop and down to a folding chair to which the rope is tied, holding the rope in place.

Students jump off on two feet and kick the ball with one foot and land on one foot. Safety and careful judgment must be used. Students should land on one foot with a bent knee.

15. Lacrosse

Equipment:

- 10-12 scoops
- 1 whiffle ball per game
- Cones to mark the goals

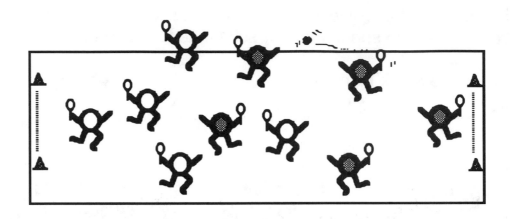

Description of the Activity: Using two teams of 5-6, students pass the ball using the scoops to score goals. If there are extra players, rotate the new players in every 2-3 minutes.

16. Jacks or Arm Wrestling

Equipment:
- Sets of jacks with balls
- Mats

Description of the Activity: The students can choose a partner to participate in either a game of jacks or an arm wrestling match. The arm wrestling is done on a tumbling mat. Vinyl tape/floor tape can be used to mark the arm positions.

17. Pony Race

Equipment:
- 4 scooters
- 4 cones

Description of the Activity: This activity is done in relay formation. Divide the class into four teams. Scooters are used as the ponies. Students must keep hands from the edges of the scooters. On the signal to begin, the first students in each line go forward or backward to the cone and back to the starting line. The scooter is given to the next person in line who repeats the activity.

Great Relay Field Day

"Great Relay" Field Day

Background: The Great Relay Field Day is somewhat different from a tradtional half-day or full-day event. This field day is designed so that students from each grade level participate for a 45-minute period. Here is a sample schedule for our classes:

8:30 - 9:15	Sixth Grade
9:30 - 10:15	Fifth Grade
10:30 - 11:15	Fourth Grade
11:30 - 12:15	Third Grade
12:30 - 1:15	Second Grade
1:30 - 2:15	First Grade

Format: This format can accommodate up to seven classes per grade level. Each class is assigned to a beginning station and rotates to the other stations during the 45-minute period. We have at least one more relay station than there are classes in each grade level, so there is never a class waiting to participate.

Each of the classes is divided into **four groups**. These four groups participate in a relay race at each of the **eight** stations. They will stay in the same group the entire time they are outside. Teachers help to get each group into single-file lines behind the designated cone or chair. After each class has completed a relay, they move to another one. If there is still some time left, classes may select any of them to repeat.

Parent Volunteers: Each station has one or two parent volunteers to explain the relay. The teachers are asked to reinforce the parent volunteers' directions and to encourage fair play among the teams.

Field Day Certificates: We do not give 1st, 2nd, or 3rd place ribbons, because "everyone is a winner" at Great Relay Field Day! Students receive certificates which are handed out before going home. All of our teachers are encouraged to come dressed to participate. The children love to see them out there having fun too!

1. **The USA Relay**

   Equipment:
   - 4 chairs or cones (used as the starting point)
   - 4 pencils and outline maps of US (4 per class)
   - 4 small frisbees
   - Large map of the United States

   Description of the Activity: This activity takes advantage of the large map of the United States painted on our outdoor basketball court. The teams stand in single-file lines behind a chair on either side of the large map. Each team has a pencil and a map on the chair. On the signal to begin, the first player on each team throws the small frisbee onto the map and works together with his team to decide which state the frisbee has landed on. The thrower labels the state, then retrieves the frisbee and gives it to the next person in line. Continue until 10 states are correctly labeled. (The teacher/parent volunteer will have a "key.") If a team accomplishes this fairly quickly, challenge them to see how many more states they can name.

2. **The Recycle Relay**

   Equipment:
   - 4 chairs or cones (used as the starting point)
   - 8 boxes - (4 of them filled with recyclable items)

   Description of the Activity: The teams line up single file behind a cone or chair. On the signal to begin, the first player runs to the recycle box, brings back one item to be recycled and places it in his team's box, then goes to the back of the line. Continue until all items are removed from the recycle box. Reverse the procedure to return items to the recycle box.

   Teacher Note: Try throwing in some items that are not recyclable!! Challenge the students to choose only the correct items from the recycle box!

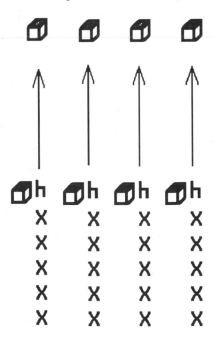

3.   The Bat Spin Relay

Equipment: • 4 chairs or cones (used as the starting point)
• 4 plastic bats
• 4 hula hoops

Description of the Activity: The teams
line up single file behind a cone or chair.
On the signal to begin, the first person in
each line runs to the bat, stands it up on
end, puts his forehead on the end of the
bat, and runs around it in a circle three
times. He then replaces the bat into the
hoop, runs back to his team, and goes to
the end of the line. Continue until each
person has gone three times. Repeat the
relay if there is time.

Teacher Note: Sometimes it is helpful to have "helpers" spread out
to assist those who may be "off course."

4.   The Restaurant Relay

Equipment: • 4 chairs or cones (used as the starting point)
• 4 rubber chickens and 4 potatoes
• 4 serving trays
• 20 cones placed in a zig-zag pattern (5 per team)

Description of the Activity: The teams line up single file behind a
cone or chair. The first team member places a rubber chicken and a
potato on their tray. On the signal to begin, the first player on each
team will zig-zag around the five cones and back, handing the tray to
the next person in line. That person will go to the end of the line while
the second person repeats the relay. If any items are dropped, just
stop and replace them to continue until all members of the team have
had 4-5 turns.

5. **The Tire Roll Relay**

   Equipment:
   - 8 chairs or cones
   - 4 tires

   Description of the Activity: The teams stand in single-file lines, behind a chair or cone. On the signal to begin, the first player for each team will roll the tire down and around the far chair and back to the next team member. One hand must remain in contact with the tire at all times. Continue until all have had a chance to run 4-5 times.

6. **The Ice Cream Cone Relay**

   Equipment:
   - 4 chairs or cones (used as the starting point)
   - 4 foam balls
   - 4 small cones

   Description of the Activity: The teams stand in single-file lines, behind a chair or cone. On the signal to begin, the first player for each team places the foam ball (ice cream) in the upside-down cone. The player runs around the chair and returns to hand the cone to the next person. If the ice cream is dropped, stop, replace it and continue. The children may not use their free hand to hold the ice cream on the cone nor may they "stuff" the ball into the cone.

7. **Indy 500 Race Cars**

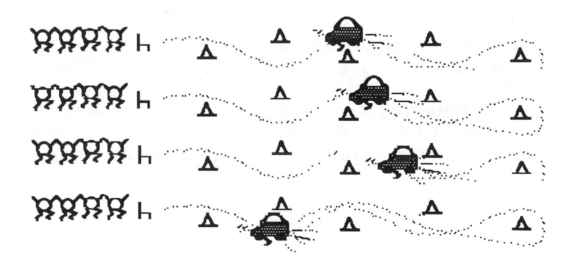

Equipment:
- 4 chairs or cones to use as a starting point
- 4 race car boxes (made from large, unfolded cardboard boxes, decorated to resemble a race car)
- 16 cones (4 per team lined up in a zig-zag pattern)

Description of the Activity: The teams stand in single-file lines, behind a chair or cone. On the signal to begin, the first player steps into the "car," lifts it up, holds the bottom edge and zig zags around the cones and back to the team. They get out of the car and give it to the next person to run the course. Continue until all have had a chance to run the course 4-5 times.

8. **The Shoe Kick Relay**

Equipment:
- 4 chairs or cones (used as the starting point)

Description of the Activity: The teams stand in single-file lines, behind a chair or cone. Have the children loosen their shoestrings and slip their foot part way out of one of their shoes before they begin so that their shoe can be easily kicked off.

On the signal to begin, the first student in each line kicks off his shoe to see how far it will go. Have the students leave the shoes on the ground, get back out of the way and continue until all of the children have had a turn to see which shoe goes the longest distance.

Teacher Note: You can also have them kick, retrieve their shoe, go to the back of the line, and continue having contests among the four players rather than the entire group. Repeat several times.

Color Team Field Day

"Color Team" Field Day

Background: The Color Team Field Day is named for our school's colors. In this field day, the students are divided into the Red Team and the Blue Team. The students compete to earn points for their "color team" at each of the stations manned by parent volunteers.

Three Field Days: We generally have three field days. One field day is for grades 5 and 6, one is for grades 3 and 4, and one is for K-2. A map, description of events, and a score sheet are given to each teacher in advance. Each class travels from station to station as a group. The class knows where to start and they rotate around the field and gym in a prescribed manner.

Using a series of speakers in the gym and outdoors, I am able to tell the classes when to rotate to the next station. Each teacher stays with his class until the end of the five events, keeping score and helping as needed.

Our Color Teams: Each classroom teacher is asked to **divide the class into two teams - Red and Blue**. A note is then sent home advising the parents which color their child is and hopefully they can wear some article of clothing that is red or blue.

Scoring: The teacher is asked to keep track of the top three boys and top three girls in each event by time, points, or whatever measure is used to score the performance. **Please see page 62 for a sample score sheet.** At the end of the field day, I collect all of the score sheets from each class, and determine the winners of each event by grade level. We also determine the Color Team points. This is done on a 5, 3, 1 basis -- 5 points for first place, 3 for second, and 1 point for third place. Color Team points are awarded for the top three boys and the top three girls by grade level.

Certificates: We make our own certificates with "Print Artist" on red paper for the Red Team and on blue paper for the Blue Team. Ribbons can also be given for the top three boys and top three girls by grade level in each event.

Distance Run: At the end of the events, the group gathers at a designated area for the distance run. A course is about one-quarter mile around our field. There are four races on a voluntary basis. The races are for 5th grade girls, 5th grade boys, 6th grade girls, and 6th grade boys. The parents stand at various spots around the course to help guide the students, and are available if any problems occur. Ribbons are given to the first five finishers.

Third and Fourth Grade Field Day: The field day for Grades 3 and 4 is the same format as the 5th and 6th grade. The only change is that some of the events are different. There is also a Primary Grade field day at our school. This includes our Pre-1st through 2nd grades. They also do the distance run at the end for ribbons.

Field Day Schedule: The field days usually begin at 9:15 a.m. on the field with a quick meeting where we go over the format and answer any questions. Since I use the same basic schedule each year, the teachers and many of the helpers are familiar with what we do. We are almost always finished by 11:00 a.m. as we must start getting ready for lunch, and because the fields are used for recess.

The students can choose to participate or not, but most teachers greatly encourage them to choose some and/or all of the activities. If there is inclement weather, we try to reschedule the field day if there is an open date with available volunteers.

Water Break: Since it is often very hot in June, we try to have a water stop set up by the parents. The students, in recent years, have been allowed to bring water bottles, but they are under strict supervision.

Your Role: The role of the physical education teacher is that of an organizer, facilitator, and trouble shooter. I also organize the Distance Run. I try to have the results and ribbons done as soon as possible.

In Closing: We have found this to be a fun activity for our students. I like this format for our school building and outside setting.

The following station activities can be adjusted and modified as you see fit. Suggested grade levels are indicated for each station. Since the Color Team points are determined by the top three boys and the top three girls, it is generally advised to let all of the girls go first, then run the boys next. You can alternate this (boys first, girls next) from station to station.

1. **Basketball Shooting Contest (Grades 5-6)**

    Equipment: • Cones and basketballs

    Description of the Activity: There will be three cones on the basketball court. A basket made from the most distant cone will count for 5 points, from the middle cone will count for 3 points, and from the closest cone will count 1 point. Each student will get a total of five shots from any of the three cones. Record the total points for the five shots.

2. **Softball Throw and Go (K-6)**

    Equipment: • Cones and softballs
    • Tape measure and beanbags to mark the throws

    Description of the Activity: Use the cones to mark off the throwing area and distances. Have four students throw at the same time. Each student is given a numbered softball. They must throw the ball as far as they can, mark the three longest throws with a beanbag, then bring the ball back to the throwing line. This continues as the next four students throw and move the beanbags (as necessary) to mark the top three throws.

3. **Soccer Dribble Obstacle Course Race (K-6)**

    Equipment: • Soccer balls
    • Obstacles to dribble around: tires, cones, etc.
    • Stopwatch

    Description of the Activity: The students must dribble the soccer balls around the tires and cones and back to the starting line. Record the top three scores.

4.   **The Twins Race (K-6)**

Equipment: • Wands
 • Cones
 • Stopwatch

Description of the Activity: This race is
done with two people. They line up at
the starting line back-to-back with a wand
between their legs. Holding onto the
wand, they run to the turning line
(marked by the cones), one going forward, the other backward. When they
cross the turning line they reverse and go
back to the finish line. Record the top three times.

5.   **Softball Accuracy Throwing Contest (Grades 5-6)**

Equipment: • Softballs
 • 2 barrels (or trash cans)

Description of the Activity: The students form two lines behind second base. The two barrels (or trash cans) are set up on either side of
home plate. Standing behind the base, each thrower is given three
attempts to throw his ball into the barrel. Awards 5 points if the ball
goes in the barrel, 3 if it hits the barrel, and 1 point if it hits the barrel
after more than one bounce. Record the top three scores.

6.   **Basketball Wall Volley Contest (Grades 3-4)**

Equipment: • Basketballs
 • Gym tape
 • Stopwatch

Description of the Activity: The students will stand behind a line in
the gym. They must throw the ball above the horizontal line marked
on the wall without crossing the line on the floor. They will have 30
seconds to see how many times they can throw and catch the basketball. Record the top three scores.

7.   **220-Yard Run (Grades 3-4)**

> **Equipment:** • Cones to mark the course
>   • Stopwatches

> **Description of the Activity:** Run heats of 5-6 students. The top two girls and boys advance to the final heats. On the last heats, time and record the top three.

8.   **The Golf Ball Race (K-2)**

> **Equipment:** • Golf balls
>   • Spoons
>   • Stopwatches

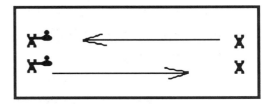

> **Description of the Activity:** Each class will separate into its Red and Blue teams. Divide the teams into groups of two players. One partner lines up on the left side of the playing area holding a golf ball with a spoon. The other partner waits on the right side of the playing area. The spoon must be held in one hand only. If the ball falls, the runner must stop and replace the ball on the spoon. When the student gets to the other side, the golf ball and spoon are given to the partner. The partner quickly walks/runs back to the other side to complete the race. Race two partners at a time. Record the top three times.

9.   **Sack Race (K-2)**

> **Equipment:** • Cones (to mark the playing area) and burlap sacks
>   • Stopwatches

> **Description of the Activity:** Each class will separate into its Red and Blue teams. Divide the teams into groups of two players. One partner lines up on the left side of the playing area with the sack. The student jumps to his teammate on the opposite side. When the student gets to the other side, the sack is given to the partner who jumps back to the starting line. Race two partners at a time. Record the top three times.

10. The Disk Race (K-2)

Equipment: • Red and blue disks made from construction paper
• Stopwatches

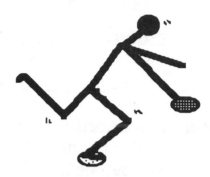

Description of the Activity: Each class will separate into its Red and Blue teams. Divide the teams into groups of two players. One partner lines up on the left side of the playing area with a red and a blue disk. They place one disk on the ground and step on it with one foot. They then repeat the action by placing the other disk on the ground and stepping on it. The object of this activity is to move toward their partner by picking up the trailing disk and putting it forward. When the student gets to the other side, the two disks are given to the partner who goes back to the other side. Race 3-4 partners at a time. Record the top three times.

11. The Clothing Race (K-2)

Equipment: • Old clothes placed in large paper bags
• Stopwatches

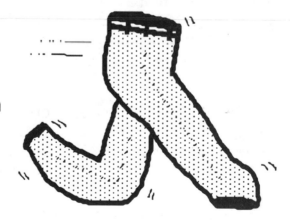

Description of the Activity: Each class will separate into its Red and Blue teams. Divide the teams into partners. One partner lines up on the left side of the playing area with the bag. When the race starts, the first child puts on all the clothes in his bag, runs to the other side of the area and removes the clothes which his teammate must put on. The clothes will consist of oversize shirts, pants, and socks to be worn over the child's own clothes and shoes. The partner may help with the clothing. Race 3-4 partners at a time. Record the top three times.

12. **The Distance Race (K-6):** This race, of a length to be determined, will be held if time and conditions permit. It will be on an individual basis and ribbons are given to the first eight places. We give out ribbons for boys and girls for each grade level.

   Equipment:
   - Cones to mark the course
   - Stopwatches

Sample Score Sheet: Shown below is a sample score sheet for 5th-6th grade. Please note that the score cards for grades K-2 and 3-4 would have different events listed.

Classroom Teacher: _____ Grade: _____

1.) Basketball Shooting:

Girls - Winner's Name	Score	Color Team:
1. _____	_____	_____
2. _____	_____	_____
3. _____	_____	_____

1.) Basketball Shooting:

Boys - Winner's Name	Score	Color Team:
1. _____	_____	_____
2. _____	_____	_____
3. _____	_____	_____

2.) Softball Throw:

Girls - Winner's Name	Score	Color Team:
1. _____	_____	_____
2. _____	_____	_____
3. _____	_____	_____

2.) Softball Throw:

Boys - Winner's Name	Score	Color Team:
1. _____	_____	_____
2. _____	_____	_____
3. _____	_____	_____

3.) Soccer Dribble:

Girls - Winner's Name	Score	Color Team:
1. _____	_____	_____
2. _____	_____	_____
3. _____	_____	_____

3.) Soccer Dribble:

Boys - Winner's Name	Score	Color Team:
1. _____	_____	_____
2. _____	_____	_____
3. _____	_____	_____

4.) Twins Race:

Girls - Winner's Names	Score	Color Team:
1. _____	_____	_____
2. _____	_____	_____
3. _____	_____	_____

4.) Twins Race:

Boys - Winner's Name	Score	Color Team:
1. _____	_____	_____
2. _____	_____	_____
3. _____	_____	_____

5.) Softball Accuracy Throw:

Girls - Winner's Name	Score	Color Team:
1. _____	_____	_____
2. _____	_____	_____
3. _____	_____	_____

5.) Softball Accuracy Throw:

Boys - Winner's Name	Score	Color Team:
1. _____	_____	_____
2. _____	_____	_____
3. _____	_____	_____

Super Kids Field Day

"Super Kids" Field Day

Background: The "Super Kids" Field Day is non-stop fun! While this 34-station event requires plenty of parent volunteers, materials, and planning, it is the "highlight" of the school year.

To begin, all of the **students are given a partner** by the classroom teacher. The partners have a "Passport Card" and move from station to station as they wish. Once they have participated at a station, the parent volunteer marks the "Passport Card" with a colored marker.

Station Set-Up: Each station parent volunteer needs a clipboard and a marker. Each station should be equipped and have a chair for the parent to sit in, as needed. **Students are on their own.** When they come to a station, they get in line. There should be no more than 10 students waiting in line at a time. Otherwise, the extra students go to another station.

Why We Do It This Way: In the past, all of our field days used the traditional field day events of running, throwing, relays, etc. Often the same students were always winning, so we went with this format and the response has been fantastic! I'm even having former elementary students coming back the last week of school when they are done with their semester tests and helping at the stations. We use them as "floaters" to give the teachers and volunteers breaks.

FIELD DAY PASSPORT

Issued to: _____ & _____

1	2	3							
4	5	6	7	9	10	11	12	13	14
15	16	17	18	19	20	21	22	23	24
25	26	27	28	29	30	31	32	33	34

Activity Descriptions: The following activities are organized in a way so that the children are spread out, move at their own pace, have a chance to interact with other grade levels, and work with many different partners. Fun is the idea and each activity encourages all helpers, staff and children to have a super day!

1. **Grocery Shopping**

    Equipment:
    - 2 long coats
    - 2 hats
    - 2 grocery sacks
    - 2 boxes of groceries
    - 2 hula hoops

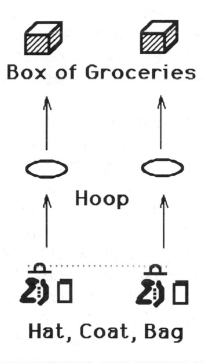

Box of Groceries

Hoop

Hat, Coat, Bag

Description of the Activity: As stated in the background information, the student partners compete against each other at each of the stations. On the signal to begin, each student puts on a long coat and hat. They will then pick up a grocery sack and run to their hoop to place the sack in the middle. Next, they will run to the box filled with groceries and take one item out to run back to the sack and place it in the bag. This continues until all items from the basket are in the sack. Then the students will pick up the grocery bag and run back to the starting line. The first student back is the winner.

2. **Balloon Mash**

    Equipment:
    - 2 bags of balloons
    - 2 chairs

Description of the Activity: On the signal to begin, each student runs to where the balloons are waiting, picks one up, runs back to the starting line, and sits on the balloon until it pops.

3. Sponge Toss

Equipment:
- 1 jug per team
- 1 sponge per team
- 1 bucket of water per team

Description of the Activity: With a partner, the students will compete with other groups of students to fill up a jug with water. On the signal to begin, the student next to the bucket of water dips the sponge in the water and tosses it to his partner. This student will wring out the water into the jug and toss the dry sponge back. Continue until one team has filled the jug up to the designated line.

4. Hula-hoop Jive

Equipment:
- 1 hula hoop per person

Description of the Activity: Each student competes with one other student by trying to keep the hula hoop spinning the longest. The hoops should be spun around the waist and no hands should be used. Be sure to have plenty of space between students so they will not interfere with others.

5. Hammer Pound

Equipment:
- 1 railroad tie
- 1 hammer per student
- 1 nail per student

Description of the Activity: On the signal to begin, each student picks up a nail and begins to hammer the nail into the railroad tie. If the nail bends, use the claw to straighten it out. The first student to pound his nail into the railroad tie is the winner. Stress safety at this station!

6. Beanbag Toss

Equipment:
- Beanbags
- Handmade cardboard targets

Description of the Activity: Each student will have a chance to toss one beanbag toward the targets that are placed on the ground. The student who gets the closest to the bull's eye wins.

7. Frisbee Toss

Equipment:
- 2 frisbees
- 1 hula hoop extended above the ground
- Handmade cardboard target

Description of the Activity: The first student will toss the frisbee toward the hula hoop and try to get it through or nearest to the target. The student who gets the closest to the bull's eye wins.

8. Ring Toss

Equipment:
- 2 hula hoops
- 1 large cone

Description of the Activity: The first student will take a hula hoop and toss it toward the large cone. One hoop is thrown at a time. The person who can ring the most cones is the winner. If no hoops ring the cones, the person closest wins.

9. Shoe Kick

Equipment:
- Two cones for a starting line

Description of the Activity: The students will loosen the shoelaces of one shoe and place the shoe loosely back on their feet. One step is taken before letting the shoe fly. The shoe that goes the longest distance is the winner.

10. Tricycle Race

Equipment:
- 2 tricycles
- 4 cones for starting and ending lines

Description of the Activity: On the signal to begin, the students will sit on the tricycle and pedal. They will race to the far cones with the first one over the line declared the winner.

11. Hoppity Hop

Equipment:
- 2 hoppity hops
- 4 cones for starting and ending lines

Description of the Activity: On the signal to begin, each student will sit on the hoppity hop and, using a jumping action, race their hoppity hop to the finish line. The first person across the line is the winner.

12. Gunny Sack Race

Equipment:
- 2 sacks
- 4 cones for starting and ending lines

Description of the Activity: Step into the sack and stand at the starting line. On the signal to begin, the students jump toward the finish line. The first to cross the line with the sack still on is the winner.

13. Short Sprint

Equipment:
- 4 cones for starting and finishing lines
- Stopwatch

Description of the Activity: On the signal to begin, the students will run 50 yards to the finish line. Record the heat winners and let them run a final race to determine an overall winner.

14. **Tire Roll**

    Equipment: • 1 tire for each pair of students
    • 4 cones for starting and finishing lines

    Description of the Activity: Two students will hold the tire up and race against another pair of students. On the signal to begin, they will roll the tire toward the finish line. When they cross the line they need to sit down with their own tire. A variation on this would be to tie a rope around the tire and tie the other end around the waist of one student. These students would then race down to the finish line dragging the tire behind them.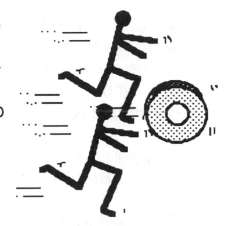

15. **Soccer Kick**

    Equipment: • Soccer balls

    Description of the Activity: Two students will compete with each other. On the signal to begin, each student will pick up the soccer ball and kick it for distance. The ball that lands farthest from the starting point is the winner. Players should retrieve the balls.

16. **Balloon Toss**

    Equipment: • Water balloons

    Description of the Activity: Students should be partnered. Each pair of students is given a water balloon. The couples toss the balloons back and forth during the time given. After the balloon is tossed to the partner and it does not break, the person with the balloon steps back one step. This continues until there is only one pair of students left.

17. 3-Legged Race

Equipment:
- Old bedsheets cut into strips. You can also use car tire inner tubes cut into 2"-3" bands.
- 4 cones to be the starting and ending lines

Description of the Activity: Students need to get into partners and tie the cloth strip around their ankles. On the signal to begin, the partners work together to run to the finish line. When they have crossed the line, they need to sit down.

18. Tennis Ball Carry

Equipment:
- 1 racquetball per partner
- 1 tennis racquet per partner
- 4 cones for each partner

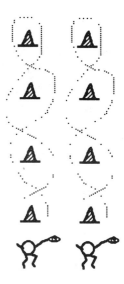

Description of the Activity: Two students will compete with each other. On the signal to begin, each student picks up a tennis racquet and places a racquetball on top. Each student will then race through the cones in a figure-eight weave and back to the starting line. If the ball drops, the student must replace it on the racquet and begin where the ball fell.

19. Watercup Relay

Equipment:
- 1 cup with a pin hole in the bottom per team
- 1 jug per team
- 1 large bucket full of water

Description of the Activity: On the signal to begin, the first student on each team fills the cup with water and runs down to put the water in the jug. This student will run back and pass the cup on to the next person in line. Continue until the jug is filled to the water line.

20. Football Throw

Equipment: • Footballs

Description of the Activity: Each student will have a chance to throw the football as far as possible. The one who throws the football the farthest is the winner.

21. Highland Games Caber Toss

Equipment: • Swimming pool "Noodles"

Description of the Activity: The caber toss is a traditional event at the Scottish Highland Games. In this event, a huge wooden pole is carried and then tossed end-over-end for distance. Each student will toss the noodle like a caber.

22. Spoon Marble Relay

Equipment: • 1 spoon per student
• 3 marbles per student
• 1 empty container per student

Description of the Activity: Two students compete with each other. On the signal to begin, each student will place a marble in the spoon, race to the other end, and drop the marble into the container. Then they run back to the starting line, get another marble and continue until all three marbles have been dropped in the container.

23. World Cup Soccer

Equipment: • Several soccer balls
• Cones to mark off the goal

Description of the Activity: Two students will compete against each other. One stands in the goalie position while the other student tries to kick the ball to score a goal. Repeat with the goalie switching positions with the first kicker.

24. Big Ball Throw

Equipment:
- 2 big balls
- 2 cones for starting line

Description of the Activity: Two students will compete against each other. One stands behind the line and tosses the big ball. The student whose ball travels the farthest distance is the winner.

25. Wheelbarrow Relay

Equipment:
- 1 wheelbarrow per team
- 1 cone per team located 20 or more yards away

Description of the Activity: On the signal to begin, the first person on each team will push the wheelbarrow down, around the cone, and back to the next person in line.

26. Ball Between Knees

Equipment:
- 1 nerf ball per team
- 1 cone for each team

Description of the Activity: On the signal to begin, the first person on each team places the nerf ball between the knees and jumps or walks to the cone and back. They must keep their hands away from the ball and if the ball drops out, pick it up and start where the ball came loose.

27. Tug-a-War

Equipment:
- 1 heavy-duty rope
- 2 cones to mark the dividing line

Description of the Activity: Two students will compete against each other. On the signal to begin, each student will pull an end of the rope and try to pull the other person across the line.

28. Super Soaker Target

Equipment:
- 2 super soakers
- 6 milk cartons
- 2 cones to designate the shooting line
- 1 bench

Description of the Activity: Two students compete against each other. Each student has a super soaker and stands behind the shooting line. On the signal to begin, they will shoot their super soaker until all three of their milk cartons are knocked off the bench.

29. Arm Wrestling

Equipment:
- 1 mat

Description of the Activity: Two students will compete against each other. Both of the students should be on their stomachs on the mat facing each other.

30. Basketball Shoot

Equipment:
- 2 basketballs
- 1 basketball hoop

Description of the Activity: Two students will compete against each other. Each student will shoot two shots at close range. Whoever makes the most baskets wins. There may need to be a time limit on this station since it will be very popular with the students.

31. Jump Rope Contest

Equipment:
- 1 jump rope per student

Description of the Activity: Each student takes a jump rope and begins to jump on the signal to begin. The person in charge can ask them to do different challenges such as one foot only, hot pepper (faster), backwards, etc. Whoever lasts the longest wins. If they both go for a long time (2 minutes or so) declare a tie.

73

32. **Under the Limbo Stick**

    Equipment: • 1 long bamboo pole
                   • Portable cassette/CD player and music

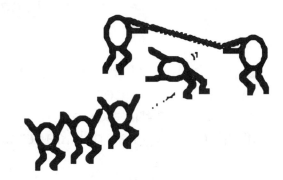

Description of the Activity:
Four to six players at a time can participate in "dancing" under the limbo stick as the music plays. Lower the stick after each round until there is only one student left.

33. **Marble Grab with Feet**

    Equipment: • 1 wading pool
                   • Bag of marbles
                   • 1 empty container per student

Description of the Activity: Two to four students will compete against each other. Each student will take off his shoes and socks. Standing in the pool, the student will pick up the marbles with his toes and place them in the container. The person who gets five marbles into his container first is the winner.

34. **Hang-up Clothes Relay**

    Equipment: • 2 tubs of water
                   • Old clothes
                   • Clothesline with clothespins

Description of the Activity: Two students at a time will start. Each student will have a tub of water with clothing in the water. On the signal to begin, each student takes one piece of clothing and carries it to the clothesline, hangs it up, and clips it with clothespins. He then runs back to get another piece until all three pieces of clothing are on the line. To finish the race, each piece of clothing must be returned to the tub and the pins put back in the bag.

Fitness Festival Field Day

"Fitness Festival" Field Day

Background: The "Fitness Festival" Field Day promotes sport and personal fitness as an important part of a healthy lifestyle. Several days before the activity we put up signs on the gym wall for each station and explain the stations to the students. Parent volunteers help to direct the stations. Included in the stations are a first aid area, the watering stations and a lost and found area. All the students will have a picnic lunch on the school grounds and certificates will be presented after the field day activities are completed.

Activity Description: These field day activities are divided into grade levels - K-2, and 3-5. This format works well for a small school where several grade levels can participate at the same time. There are eight different stations for the younger students and eight for the older students. Some of the stations have **all-group participation** and others are **individual challenges**. The emphasis for these activities should be a non-competitive approach. All students can achieve at their own level!

K - Second Grade Stations	Third - Fifth Grade Stations
1. Parachute Works	1. Home Run Derby
2. Sprint Nationals	2. Cooperation Challenges
3. Toss and Catch	3. 5 Goal Soccer
4. Zookeeper Game	4. Target Volleyball
5. Super Soccer	5. Australian Beanbag Steal
6. Marvin K. Mooney Relay	6. Race for the States
7. Ball Hunt	7. Sockball Horseshoes
8. Ready? Aim... Throw!	8. Can We Throw a Mile?

1. **Parachute Works (K-2)**

    Equipment: • 1 parachute
    • Yarn balls

    Directions: The following directions are to be given by the parent volunteer to the students:

    "We need to be super listeners! We can work together to make the parachute do special things. Spread out around the parachute, hold it with both hands at waist level."

    Ripples & Waves - Hold the parachute at waist level and move your hands up and down. To make larger waves, move the arms up and down.

    The Bubble - Let's count 1,2,3, together, then lift our arms up high. Keep your arms up! Count 1,2,3 up and take two steps toward the center. Repeat a couple of times to make sure everyone is working together. After we lift the parachute, I will call a color. If I call the color you are wearing, let go of the parachute, run to the center and back to your original space. Grab hold of the parachute as it comes down.
    • Can you shake hands with someone while under the parachute?
    • Can you give someone a high five while under the parachute?

    Submarines - Count off by 4's around the parachute. This will give you four groups. After we count to 3 and lift the parachute, I will call a number. Those "submarines" let go of the parachute, leave their port, cross under the ocean and dock on the other side!

    Merry-Go-Round - Everyone holds the parachute with their right hand. They walk around with the parachute in a clockwise direction and stop on the signal. Then they change to their left hands and walk in the other direction until they hear the signal to stop and reverse directions again. Try skipping or galloping too!

<u>Race Around the Clock</u> - This is played with one-half of the class at a time. Just like the merry-go-round, hold the parachute with the right hand and pull tight. Choose a leader or a home spot. The whole group will run around as fast as they can for 30 seconds. Count how many times the leader passes the home spot.

<u>Popcorn</u> - Place balls on the parachute. Make waves and try to toss all the balls off the parachute as quickly as you can. Pick up the balls and try again.

2. **Sprint Nationals (K-2)**

    Equipment: • 4 tires
                         • 4 to 16 cones
                         • 4 cardboard cars (with rope handles)

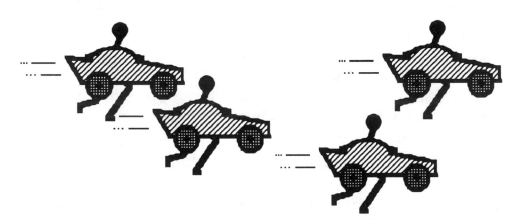

Directions: Divide the class into four groups mixing girls and boys as equally as possible. Each group lines up behind the cones, relay style. Point out the tire that is in front of each group. Demonstrate how to hold the cardboard car before starting the race. Each person will have a turn to race with the "car" around the tire, back to the next person in line and then moves to the end of the line. The race will last for 3 minutes. Please keep track of how many "laps" each group completes in 3 minutes. You can add cones to race around before going around the tire.

3.   **Toss & Catch (K-2)**

   Equipment: • Crab-shaped beanbags
                    • Koosh balls
                    • Objects that represent "fish"
                    • 1 bucket per group

   Activity: Divide the class into three equal groups. Each group will rotate to the three tossing and catching activities.

   1 - Play catch with a crab! This is a partner
       activity using beanbags in the shape of a crab. Play
       catch, moving further away after four successful catches.

   2 - Toss the fish into the bucket! A bucket is
       placed a few feet away from the starting line. Using
       an object that represents the fish, each person has a
       chance to toss the fish into the bucket.

   3 - Play catch with a sea urchin! With a partner
       standing a determined distance away, toss the koosh
       ball back and forth without dropping it.

4.   **Zookeeper Game (K-2)**

   Equipment: • 2 or 3 hula hoops at each end of the playing area

   Activity: This is a running, chasing, fleeing game that takes place in the zoo! Ask the children which are their favorite animals at the zoo. As they play this game, they might want to imitate this animal. The animals are all loose, and the zookeepers are trying to catch them and put them back in their cages!

   Choose two students to be the zookeepers. They try to tag the flee-ing students ("animals") softly and carefully on the back or shoulder with a two-finger touch. If tagged, the animals go to a cage represent-ed by a hoop and squat down inside. Other students can set the animals free by lifting up the "cage door." This is done by picking up the hula hoop and bringing it over the head of the caught animal.   Play about two minutes and stop to change the zookeepers. Always check for untied shoelaces between rounds of the game. Take time if need-ed between rounds to rest. This would be a good time to give every-one a sticker of a zoo animal, or an animal cracker!

5.   Super Soccer (K-2)

Equipment: • Soccer goal
• 8 soccer balls (4 per dribbling activity)
• 16 or more cones
• 4 boxes
• 4 hula hoops

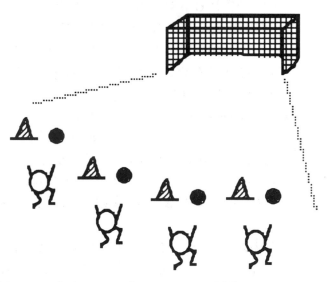

Activity: Divide the class in half with a mixture of boys and girls on even teams. One group starts with a shooting activity while the other half is involved in a dribbling activity. Rotate the groups after 5 minutes.

Shooting for Accuracy: The students line up in four sin-gle-file lines behind the cones and run to kick the ball toward the goal to score. When each student has gone, he retrieves his ball, and puts it back on the line for the next person.

Dribbling for Control: This dribble maze is set up in a circle. Arrange four small groups around a large circle marked by cones. The stu-dents dribble between the cones, around the hoops in the maze, and finally kick their balls into the boxes located within the center of the maze. The students should follow the circle moving in a clockwise di-rection until they get back to their group. As they maneuver the maze, students are allowed to move past students in front of them.

6. **Marvin K. Mooney Will You Please Go Now! (K-2)**

   Equipment:
   - 8 hula hoops
   - 4 beanbags
   - <u>Marvin K. Mooney Will You Please Go Now</u> by Dr. Seuss
   - 4 clipboards, pencils and papers with "Go" printed over and over on them

Activity: Divide the class into four groups. Each group lines up behind a hoop. The first person sits in the hoop; all others sit behind the hoop. There is an empty hoop in front of each team. The first person in line has a beanbag in his hand. The parent volunteer will read the story to the class. It helps to read slowly and dramatically. Each time the first students in line hear the word "Go" as the story is read, they run to the hoop in front of them, place the beanbag inside the hoop and run back

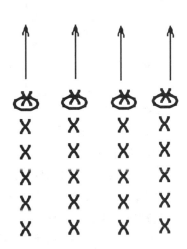

to the end of their line. The next student will retrieve the beanbag when the word "Go" is read again and bring it back to the first hoop.

At the end of each line is a clipboard, paper and pencil. Each student should cross out a "Go" on the paper each time they go to the end of the line. After the book has been finished, one student from each team should count the number of crossed-out "Go's" on their paper. Then the class can look at the book with the parent volunteer and count the number of times the word "Go" appears (38 times).

7. **Ball Hunt (K-2)**

   Equipment:
   - Bag of tennis balls that have either a vowel, consonant, or number marked on them
   - 6 hula hoops
   - 6 fun noodles

Activity: The tennis balls are scattered out on the field. Divide the class into six groups. Each group has a hoop as home base and a fun noodle to hold. In this relay, each team will be picking up tennis balls as a group and returning them to their hoop. On the signal to begin, each member of the group holds the fun noodle with one hand and runs around collecting the tennis balls with the other hand. When each person has picked up one, the group can return to the hoop and place the tennis balls inside.

The groups have 2 minutes to pick up as many balls as they can. On the signal to stop, the groups go back to their home base and count how many balls they have collected. Ask the children to look at the balls and figure out the three categories they have: numbers, vowels, consonants. Give each team 1 point for every consonant, 3 points for each vowel, and the face value for any balls with numbers written on them.

8.   **Ready? Aim ... Throw! (K-2)**

Equipment: • 12 whiffle balls
• 4 baseball mitts (large cardboard baseball mitt with a cut-out circle in the center)
• 4 basketballs and 4 goals
• 4 hula hoops
• 12 cones
• 12 beanbags (chickens) per team
• 4 buckets

Activity: Divide the class into four groups, rotating them through the four target games. The students stay at the target until the signal to move to the next game.

Target Game #1 - Baseball Mitt: Each member will throw three whiffle balls through the hole of the baseball mitt which is set up 6 feet away. That same student will pick up the balls, give them to the next person, and go the end of the line. Continue until all members of the group have thrown the balls.

Target Game #2 - Basketball: Using two hands, the first member of the group will throw the ball into the basketball hoop. After each attempt, the member will retrieve the ball to hand off to the next member.

Target Game #3 - Catch a Lobster/Crab: The first member of the group will toss the hoop toward one of the three lobsters/crabs (cones) placed in front of the line.

Target Game #4 - Bucket Toss/Chickens: Each member will have three chances to toss the chickens (beanbags) into the bucket. The bucket should be far enough away from the starting line to make it a challenge.

3-5 Stations

1.   **Home Run Derby (3-5)**

   Equipment: • 4-6 batting tees and tennis balls
   • Bats of different sizes and weights
   • Cones

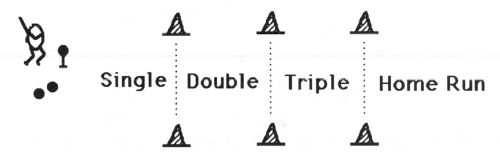

Activity: Each person will have several turns to hit the ball. The distance of the hit is determined as a single, double, triple and home run! Divide the class into lines behind the available tees. Line up behind the line and wait there for your turn at bat. You may choose the bat you would like to use. When you are batting, hold the bat with two hands at all times. Hit three balls before placing the bat on the ground, then retrieve your three balls from the field.

2. Cooperation Challenges (3-5)

Equipment:
- 6 buckets
- 12 hoops
- Tennis balls
- Frisbees

Activity: Students will be challenged to work as a team. Start with groups of three people and add another group of three as students experience success.

Game #1 - Bunny Hop: Students form a long line, one in front of the other. Each student holds the waist of the person in front of him. The entire team must jump to the designated line without breaking the chain. Start over if the chain is broken.

Hint: Take small jumps, find a rhythm, and know when to jump.

Game #2 - Sandwich: Form a long line, side by side. Students place a frisbee between their upper arm and the upper arms of their neighbors. The entire team must walk to the designated line without breaking the chain (dropping a frisbee). Forward on the first try, backwards on the second try.

Hint: Take small steps, find a rhythm, and know when to take a step.

Game #3 - Fire Bucket Relay: Divide into three groups, spreading out across the area. The first person has the fire bucket and scoops a tennis ball into it. The tennis balls represent water. Pass the fire bucket to the next person in line until it reaches the last person. The last person empties the fire bucket into the hoop and begins to pass the bucket back up the line. Continue until all the water has been passed. Hand the bucket to the next person - DO NOT THROW IT! If there is time, change places in the line and repeat from the opposite direction.

3. **5 Goal Soccer (3-5)**

Equipment: • 5 different colored soccer balls
• 10 cones (2 cones per color)
• Construction paper tickets
• Scrimmage vests (5 different colors)

Activity: Divide the class into five teams. There will be five goals spread out in a large circle. Each goal will be a different color. The object of the game is for the forwards on your team to score a goal in the four other goals excluding your own goal. Each team gets scrimmage vests corresponding to their goal, a ball, and a set of like-colored 'tickets' made from construction paper. Each player is assigned a position.

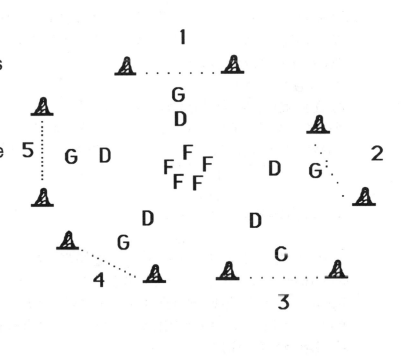

Your team must have one goalie, one defender, one forward, and one ticket keeper; any extra players may be defenders. Positions will be changed after every game. Teams are set up by their goals. The game begins with all the forwards in the center of the playing area.

On the signal to begin, the forwards dribble the soccer ball to any team goal. When a player scores a goal against a team, he earns a colorful ticket corresponding to that team. When the forward collects one ticket from each team, excluding his own, he returns to the center, shows the referee the tickets, and the game is over. Play will resume after players have rotated positions.

4.   **Target Volleyball (3-5)**

> **Equipment:** • Volleyballs
> • 2 folding mats
> • Bucket with 10 beanbags inside of it
> • 1 hula hoop
> • Poly spots

Activity: The mats will stand on edge and form a large box (target) in the center of the circle. The poly spots will mark a circle around the target. Players will stand outside the circle facing the target. The class works together as a team to earn a collective score. Each time a student scores a point he takes a beanbag out of the bucket and places it in the hula hoop.

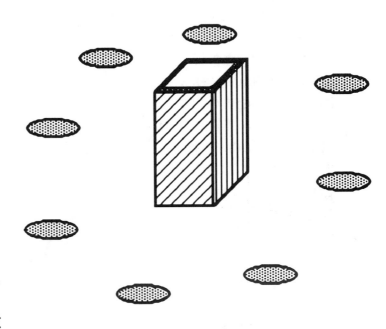

Round #1: Set - On the signal to begin, the students self-toss the volleyball and try to set it into the target. If a student "sets" the ball into the target successfully, he takes a beanbag from the bucket and places it inside the hoop. Play until there are 10 beanbags in the hoop.

Round #2: Bump - On the signal to begin, the students self-toss the volleyball and try to bump it into the target. Follow the same procedure as above. Play until 10 beanbags are in the hoop.

Round #3: Serve - On the signal to begin, the students use an underhand serve to get the ball into the target. Follow the same procedure as above. Play until 10 beanbags are in the hoop.

Round #4: Half of the class become tossers and stand with their backs to the target and face the outside of the circle facing their teammates. The tossers toss the volleyballs to their teammates, who must pass the ball into the box using the set or the bump. Play until 10 beanbags are in the hoop.

Round #5: Switch the other half of the class to tossers as above.

Teacher Tip: Grade 3 - Use Fling-it Nets. Teams of two or four students will use the nets to work together and throw as many balls as possible into the target in 3 minutes. Each team should have a few balls nearby to put on the net one at a time.

When completed, you can allow another 3 minutes for the students to try to break their previous score.

5.   Australian Beanbag Steal (3-5)

Equipment: • Hoops
• Beanbags

Activity: This is a modification of a game originating in Australia and New Zealand. Divide the class into partners. Each pair has a hoop. Partners sit behind the hoop facing the center where the beanbags have been placed.

The beanbags will be spread out so that when the first partner runs up to the pile, he won't run into anyone from the other groups. Caution the children about being careful running. The object of the game is to be the first group with three beanbags in their hoop.

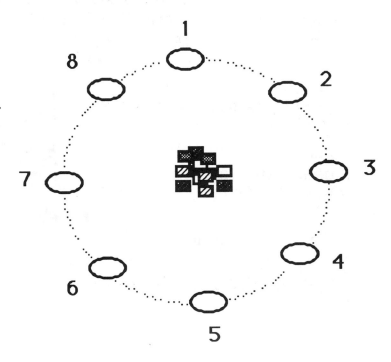

On the signal to begin, the first partner sprints to the middle, picks up a beanbag, runs back and places it in their hoop. When the beanbag is down, the second partner may leave to get a beanbag. When the pile in the center is depleted, you must take from other groups. You cannot take from players on your side! You must run across the field!

For example, Group 1 would have to take a beanbag from Groups 4, 5, 6. Group 2 could only get a beanbag from Groups 5, 6, 7. As soon as one group has three beanbags, the game is over. At this time the beanbags are returned to the center. One partner moves to the hoop to the right and everyone has a new partner as the game starts again.

6.   Race for the States (3-5)

Equipment: • 3 USA maps (showing only the outlines of the states)
• 3 containers of state cards
• 3 sets of capitals (optional)
• Master map

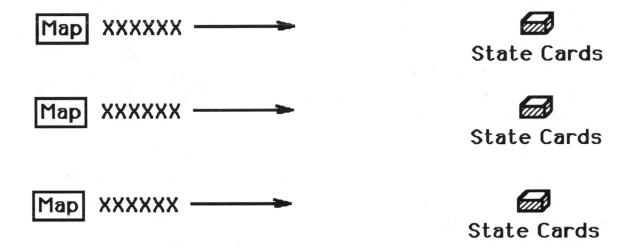

Activity: This is a relay activity in which each team will try to fill in the state names on their map. A master map is provided in order to check the accuracy of each team's work. Divide the class into three equal groups mixing girls and boys. Each group lines up relay style behind the starting line. An outline map of the USA will be behind each team.

A container of state cards will be in front of each team. On the signal to begin, the first person on each team runs to the container and picks up a state card, runs back to the team, tags the next runner, goes to the end of the line and tries to match the state with its location on the map. Teammates may help each other to match the states with their location on the map.

7. Sockball Horseshoes (3-5)

Equipment:
- Hoops
- Sockballs - 4 per game (a tennis ball inside a tube sock, tied shut)

Activity: Pairs of players will play horseshoes using sockballs and hoops as targets. Each pair of students will split up so that they face each other from opposite hoops. Each team has two sockballs. The game starts from one side. There are two teams for each hoop.

Players alternate throwing the sockball. For example:

- The first player from Team A will throw the sockball.
- The first player from Team B throws the sockball.
- The second player from Team A throws the sockball.
- Finally, the second player from Team B throws the sockball toward the hoop.

Other: Players must throw from behind the hoop. The players score points by getting the "head" (the part with the ball in it) of the sockball in the hoop. When this happens, 2 points are scored. If both sockballs are in the hoop, that earns 5 points. If none of the sockballs are in a hoop, score 1 point for the sockball that is closest to the hoop.   Play until one team reaches 7 points.

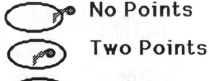

No Points

Two Points

5 Points

8.   **Can We Throw a Mile? (3-5)**

   Equipment: • Basketballs
                    • Cone markers indicating feet
                    • Clipboards & pencils
                    • Score sheets

   Activity: The scores from all students in grades 3-5 are added up to see if the distance equals a mile (5,280 feet).

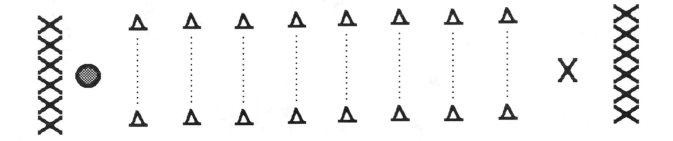

Divide the students into two groups. Groups will line up as shown. One thrower from each team will go to the starting line. The thrower may run up to the starting line and throw the basketball as far as they can using any style comfortable to them. The thrower will watch where the ball bounces and report the score to the scorekeeper, then run to the end of the other line.

Meanwhile, the first person in the other line will catch the ball after it bounces and run across the field to the throwing line. Teams must watch the thrower so that they will be ready to catch! Throwers must watch where the ball bounces and report the score to the scorekeeper.

The Bearer of this Certificate has Participated in Our Fitness Festival Field Day and is

"Fit 4 Fun!"

"We had a Ball at Our Field Day!"

_____   _____

Physical Education Teacher   Principal

Great Activities Publishing Company

School Pride Field Day

"School Pride" Field Day

Background: In our physical education classes we stress "sportsmanship with fun" as we move toward our "School Pride" Field Day. During the year, our students can earn buttons by working on the four traits of "School Pride" - effort, responsibility, caring, and teamwork.

Field Day Format: Parents, special areas teachers and paraprofessionals run the stations for the 2nd-5th grade students in the morning and 5th graders run the K-1 stations in the afternoon. We have not had any problems so far getting volunteers. Parent involvement is a big part of what makes our school special. We prepare the volunteers in advance so they will know exactly what their station will be and we also provide written directions for all of the activities.

Special Recognition: Following the field day, everyone gets a participation certificate and one class at each grade level receives a "Sportsmanship Award" which is a trophy for them to keep in their classroom.

Our classes are multi-age K/1, 2/3, and 4/5 so we give three awards. The adults that run the stations vote for the Sportsmanship Award. To help with supervision, the classroom teachers go with their classes from station to station.

What do I like best about Field Day? I enjoy seeing all the students being active at the same time; the noise of 350 laughing and cheering children is awesome! Our field day gives the whole school a great opportunity to show our school pride all at the same time as we put into practice:

Effort

Responsibility

Caring

Teamwork

Field Day Overview: Please have the station leaders stress and encourage sportsmanship at each station. A signal will sound at the end of each time slot. This is the signal to rotate to the next station. **Each class is assigned to a station**. The rotation will be in a clockwise direction and children should wait until the signal is sounded before moving to the next station. Listed below are nine different stations that we have found to be very successful with our students.

1.   **Obstacle Course**

   Equipment: • 2 stopwatches
   • Available outdoor play equipment
   • Cones, benches, hurdles, etc.

   Description: Have the students sit at a designated area and explain the course. Each child moves through the course and is timed. With two stopwatches, you can have two players running the obstacle course at a time. Give the first player about a 10-second lead, then start the second player. If you have time, they could go twice or let them go once to practice and time them on the second trip.

2.   **Tablespoon Relay**

   Equipment: • Tablespoons - one per team
   • Paper cups
   • Water buckets
   • Cones
   • Ruler

   Description: Divide the students into four or five groups and put them in lines. The first person in each line runs with a spoon to the water buckets and gets a spoonful of water. They then carefully carry the water back to their line and put it in the empty cup. Pass the spoon to the next runner. Continue for 3 -5 minutes and then measure the water. The team with the most wins!

3. **Holy Cow**

   Equipment: • Cups poked with holes
   • Cups without holes
   • 2 small buckets
   • 1 large bucket of water
   • Ruler

   Description: Divide the group into two teams and arrange students side by side. At one end of the line is a large bucket of water, and on the other end are two empty buckets. The two people closest to the bucket of water fill their cups and pass them down their line with the last person pouring any water remaining into their group's empty bucket. This player then runs to the beginning of the line, fills the cup up again and passes it down the line. Practice the relay first with the solid cups and when the students have the hang of it, change to the "hole-y" cups. After a given amount of time, the group with the most water in their bucket wins.

4. **Parachute**

   Equipment: • 1 parachute
   • Many foam balls

   Description: Review the commands for "inflating" the parachute - "1,2,3, up" to inflate and "ground" to put the parachute back down to the ground. To make a mushroom lift the parachute overhead and take three steps to the middle.

   To make an igloo, inflate the parachute and sit on the inside for the igloo. The kids enjoy trying to keep it up as long as they can. Rock back and forth on the inside of an igloo and you have the "rocking chair." Or try this - number the students by fours. By calling out a number from 1 to 4, the students with that number can quickly change places with another student.

5.   **Clothespin Tag**

Equipment: • Clothespins
                 • 4 cones to mark boundary

Description: Each student gets two clothespins and clips them to his shirt sleeve. The object of this tag game is for students to take the clothespins from others and put them on their own shirts. Students can only take one at a time, and they can go to the leader for another clothespin if they run out. Students may not cover their clothespins with their hands to keep people from taking them!

6.   **Running Bases**

Equipment: • 4 bases
                 • Stopwatch
                 • 4 baby cones to put near bases to see more easily
                 • 1 baton for each team
                 • Paper and pen

Description: Have the students line up near home plate. One student at a time goes around the bases carrying the baton and passing it off to the next runner when he crosses the plate.

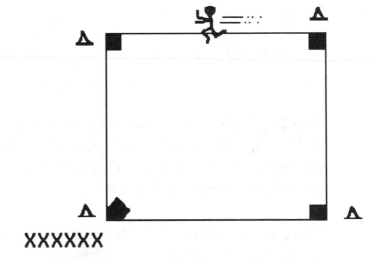

Use the stopwatch to time the whole class. Make sure each class runs 25 runners so that the times will be fair. This means that in some classes students may need to go twice.

7.   **Moon Ball**

    Equipment: • Beach balls

    Description: Divide into two groups with one beach ball per group. The task is to see how many consecutive hits the group can get before the ball hits the ground. Once a student hits the ball, he cannot hit it again until everyone has hit it. This is a group problem-solving activity and the less adult intervention the better. Encourage students to come up with ways to improve their score. For the last 5 minutes put the whole class together and set a class record. At the end of the morning we will award a certificate to the class at each grade level with the most hits.

8.   **Giant Shoes**

    Equipment: • 3 sets of "giant shoes" (Buddy Walkers)

    Description: This is a group cooperative activity. Divide the class into three groups to practice walking on the giant shoes. Remind them that it takes a lot of cooperation and teamwork to be successful on the giant shoes. After they get the hang of it, you may try a short race if time permits.

9.   **Scooter Relays**

    Equipment: • 4 scooters
                    • Beanbags
                    • Deflated balls
                    • 4 cones

    Description: Divide into four groups of students and run relays with the scooters. Some ideas for relays: backwards, sitting, on the stomach, kicking a ball, balancing a beanbag on their heads or holding it between their knees.

Great Games
Field Day

"Great Games" Field Day

Background: Here are 24 great stations that we use for our "Great Games" Field Day! Each class is divided **into two smaller groups**. Each group is assigned to one of the 24 stations.

1.   A Toy Story

Equipment:
- 4 bags filled with objects
- 1 stopwatch
- Index cards for writing down responses
- Felt markers

Activity: Various items are placed in a paper bag or box and kept out of view. Students are divided into four teams and sit in their groups. Each group is given an index card and a felt marker. On the signal to begin, the group gets 10 seconds to look into the toy bag and memorize what is inside. After the time is up, they will then write down what they can remember as quickly as they can. Give them 1 minute to write it all down. The team that has the most items recorded correctly wins. Switch bags and try again.

Hint: Students should do this quietly so they do not give away answers to other teams. Do not let anyone else see what is in the bags. Pick a recorder before they begin the round. The items should not be taken out of the bag.

2.   Grab Bag and Dash

Equipment:
- 1 beanbag per pair of students
- 1 square carpet for each beanbag

Activity: Each set of partners will sit cross-legged facing each other with hands on their knees. A beanbag is on a carpet square centered in front of the two students. On the signal to begin, they will reach for the beanbag to see who can grab it first. Try three times then switch partners. Teachers can have students on the same side move down to the next person for each new round.

3.   Team Wrap

Equipment: •   1 roll of toilet paper per class

Activity: Each class has a roll of toilet paper and tries to make a continuous wrap around the entire class without it breaking. If it breaks, they must start over from where the roll now begins. Cooperative teamwork is the key. Put all the paper in the trash can when the game is over.

4.   Obstacle Course and Dash

Equipment: •   2 folding chairs
                •   8-12 tires
                •   4 or more hurdles
                •   Several bags of balloons
                •   1 bench

Activity: Divide the group into two teams. On the signal to begin, the first student in each group puts up the folding chair, sits in it, puts it back down, runs through the tires (must put one foot in each tire, no skipping), jumps the hurdles, blows up a balloon, ties it, then sits on it until it pops. When the balloon is popped, the next member of the team starts.

5.   Wheel Relay

Equipment: •   1 baton for each team
                •   4 baseball bases

Activity: Divide the class into four teams. On the baseball diamond, the four bases are used for the starting point for each team. Each team lines up and the first person has a baton. On the signal to begin, the first person runs around the four bases and gives the baton to the next runner until the entire team has run. Move counter-clockwise. Teams should be sitting to indicate they are finished.

6. Peanut Challenge and Dash

Equipment:
- Bag of peanuts
- Mats to create 4 lanes
- Drinking straws (1 per student)
- Colored tape

Activity: On the mats there are four lanes designated by tape. In each lane is a peanut. On the signal to begin, students use a straw to blow the peanut to the finish line. Students should hold their straws until they leave this station, then discard the straws in the trash can. Four students can compete at once. Winners can have a final challenge round if time permits.

7. Indy 500 and Dash

Equipment:
- Scooter boards
- Bag of balloons
- Cones to create 4 lanes

Activity: Four race car lanes will be set up in the gym with cones as the slalom course. Each student can choose a lane. Four drivers will compete during each round. On the signal to begin, the students move their scooters through the course with their feet only. At the same time, they use their hands to bat a balloon, trying to keep it afloat. If the balloon hits the floor, they are disqualified from that heat. They can try again after everyone has had a chance.

8. **Photo Break**

   Equipment: • Instant camera
   • Water fountain

   Activity: This is a water break and a time to pose for your team picture. Smile!

9. **Waiter Relay**

   Equipment: • 1 tray per team
   • 1 cup of water per team
   • Buckets of water

XXXXXXX ———————▶ XXXXXX

XXXXXXX ———————▶ XXXXXX

Activity: Divide the group into two teams. Line up with half of the team at one side of the field. The other half lines up about 60 feet away. Fill the cup with water to the top. The first person carries the water on the tray across to the next person on their team. This person carries the tray back to the starting line to the next person. Keep going until everyone has run. If a player drops the cup from the tray, he must run to the water bucket and refill the cup.

10. **Lasso Throw**

    Equipment:

    • 2 hula hoops
    • Cartoon character
      pictures taped to 6 cones

3 Points

2 Points

1 Point

3 Points

2 Points

1 Point

Activity: Divide the group into two teams. Each team will try to capture a cartoon character by tossing the hula-hoop over a cone.
Cones are worth more points the further away they are.

11. Couch Potato Race

Equipment: • 4 small sacks of potatoes
• 4 cones

Activity: Divide the students into four teams and have them race each other while carrying the sack of potatoes to a designated finish line. Winners of each heat can race each other if time permits.

12. Jump Rope Bunch

Equipment: • 1 long jump rope
• Poster paper and markers

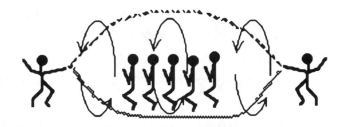

Activity: Two adults should turn the rope for this activity. The rope is turned once with one jumper inside. This person will jump only once. The next person will stand inside with the first jumper and they will jump twice. After each jump, another member of the group is added and they jump three times for three people, four times for four people, and so on. Record your highest number of jumps per class on the poster.

13. Blind Man's Bluff

Equipment: • 3 blindfolds
• 3 basketballs
• 3 basketball hoops
• Poster paper and markers

Activity: Divide students into three groups. One player from each group is blinfolded and stands on a spot near the basket. The members of the team will give him verbal cues for aiming and shooting the basketball into the hoop. Take one shot per person until everyone has had a turn. Each class records their total number of baskets made on the poster paper.

14. **50-Yard Fly By**

    Equipment: • 2 kites
                     • 4 cones

    Activity: Two students will race with their kites flying behind them. The kites should remain in the air when running through the finish line.

15. **Squeeze-It Relay**

    Equipment: • 2 soft yellow foam balls
                     • 4 cones

    Activity: Students are divided into two groups. Each group has a soft yellow foam ball. The ball is placed between the knees and each child moves up and around the cone and back any way they can without losing or touching the ball. If the ball comes out, stop and place it back between the knees before moving. When they return to their teams they hand the ball to the next person and sit at the back of the line. The team should be sitting to indicate everyone has had a turn.

16. **Clothespin Drop**

    Equipment: • 12 clothespins and two cups
                     • 2 1-liter bottles

    Activity: Each cup should have six clothespins. Students are divided into two groups. Each student takes a turn trying to drop the six clothespins into the bottle. Students must stand up straight and hold the clothespin above their waist. How many can your group make?

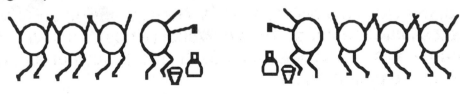

17. Treasure Chest

Equipment:
- 4 baskets
- Box filled with many items

Activity: Students are divided into four groups. Each group makes a line behind their basket. One child from each team will race to the treasure chest in the center area and pull out one item to take back to their team. The teacher may call different locomotor skills to use other than running - skipping, hopping, leaping, sliding, galloping, crab walk, etc. This can be a timed event (60 seconds) or let them go until all the treasure is gone. When completed, let each group count the number of items they have collected.

18. Sponge Lunge Relay

Equipment:
- 2 empty water buckets
- 2 full water buckets
- 1 sponge for each line

Activity: The students are in two lines facing each other. There will be a full water bucket at one end of the line and an empty bucket at the other. The first student dips the sponge into the full bucket then passes the sponge down the line.

The student at the end of the line squeezes the sponge into the empty bucket then runs back to the top of the line, dips the sponge, and passes it to the next student. This continues until all the water has been transferred or time is up. If students do not want to get wet, remind them to keep the sponge away from their body.

19. Pony Express

Equipment: • 2 stick ponies

Activity: Divide the students into two groups and have them sit in two circles. Choose a student to start and give them the "pony." The riders gallop around the outside of the circle until they get back to their starting places. They pass the pony to the next player and sit down. The two circles are racing each other to see who can finish first.

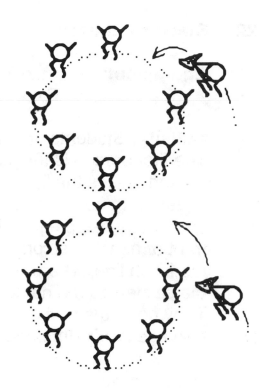

20. Magic Bubbles

Equipment: • Bottles of bubbles and wands

Activity: Children take turns making bubbles with the wand. This is also a rest stop.

21. Alligator Relay

Equipment: • 2 scooters
• 4 cones

Activity: Students are divided into two groups and line up as shown. Using the scooters, students lay on their stomachs and use both hands to propel themselves them along the floor. Remind them not to let their hands get too close to the scooter so they do not run over their fingers. They should race around the cone and back to their team.

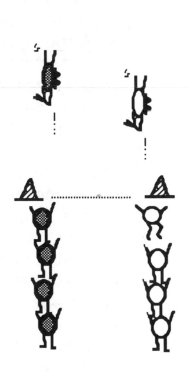

22. Stepping Stones

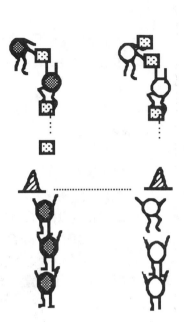

Equipment:
- 4 cones
- 3 carpet squares per team

Activity: Students are divided into two lines. The first person is the jumper and the second person places the "stepping stones" (carpet squares) in front of the first person, who moves forward by stepping on the stones placed in front of him. This continues until they reach the finish line, where they run back and return the carpets to the next two people in line. They go to the end of the line to wait for their turn again. On their next turn, they change positions.

23. Skin the Cat

Equipment:
- 1 to 2 large jump ropes

Activity: Two adults should turn the rope. Two ropes can be used for larger classes. The class forms a line and follows the leader as he runs through the rope as it is turning. No jumping, just try to run through without getting caught! See how many children can get through before someone is caught.

24. Walk of Fame

Equipment:
- Sidewalk Chalk
- Sidewalks

Activity: At this station the students are allowed to write their names and place their handprints and footprints on our "Walk of Fame." Students use the colored sidewalk chalk to draw a line around their hands and/or feet.

World Records Field Day

"World Records" Field Day

Background: During this field day, each class rotates from station to station. Parent volunteers are at each station to help explain the activity to the students. With help from the classroom teacher, the students are challenged to set a new "world's record." We conduct two field days - one for grades K-2 and one for grades 3-5.

"World Records" Field Day

We generally have our field days in the afternoon. Here's an idea of our schedule:

Time:	Activity:
12:45 PM	**Grand March:** "Let the festival begin!" The principal leads all of the students in a "pledge" in which the children state that they will abide by the rules, cooperate with others, and be respectful of others.
12:55 PM	**Ecology Race:** All of the students participate in this quick "clean-up" of the field day areas.
1:10 - 2:50 PM	**Field Day Stations:** Each class is assigned to one of ten stations. The classes rotate to the next station every 10 minutes. Here's a sample schedule for a class beginning at the "Pharaoh's Revenge" station:

1:10 PM	• Pharaoh's Revenge
1:20 PM	• That's Using Your Head
1:30 PM	• Cooperative Get Up
1:40 PM	• Continuous Dribble
1:50 PM	• All Aboard
2:00 PM	• Long, Long Jump
2:10 PM	• Distance Throwing
2:20 PM	• Feet it to Beat It
2:30 PM	• Bean Bag Balancing
2:40 PM	• The School Song

2:50 PM	**End of Field Day: Return to class.**

Ecology Race This is done to get the field ready for our two afternoon field days. We usually have our K-2 students on the first day and our 3-5 students on the second day. Our K-2 students really love doing this! They usually do such a good job that there is no need to do it with the 3-5 students.

Equipment:
- 1 plastic trash bag per class
- Enough paper bags for each pair of partners
- Bathroom scale
- Trash can

Activity: The goal of this game is to prepare a safe and a more attractive environment. Each class has one plastic trash bag. Each player may carry a paper bag or share one with a friend. On the signal to begin, each class has 3 minutes to pick up any type of litter or debris located in the games area. Anything that doesn't fit into the playground's natural environment (sticks, rocks, glass, metal, paper) is free game. Total pounds recovered will be recorded for the record.

Field Day Stations

Background: At the end of each rotation, **a student from each class will run to the scorer's table with the class score**. These class scores are added together for a cumulative score. The cumulative scores are listed on a chalkboard near the scorer's table. Also posted are the "world records" for each event. For example:

Pharaoh's Revenge: **148 points** after 6 rotations	"World Record" is **210 points.**

We have two or three parents at the scorer's table, including a representative (another parent) from Guinness' Book of World Records who even speaks with a British accent. At the end of each rotation, the Guinness representative will announce the cumulative score. The students really get excited as the cumulative score begins to get closer to the "world record." A suggested "world's record" is listed for each activity. Please feel free to adjust this figure for your students' skill level.

1. **Pharaoh's Revenge**

K-2 "World Record" is	3-5 "World Record" is
160 points.	**210 points.**

Equipment: • Tumbling mats or grass area

Activity: The goal is for the entire class to build the world's largest two-tier pyramid. The students forming the base must be on their hands and knees, shoulder to shoulder. Those on the top must also be on hands and knees with weight evenly distributed on the shoulders and hips of the bases. The complete pyramid must be held long enough to say the school name three times in order to count as a successful attempt. One point is awarded for each player participating in the pyramid.

2. **That's Using Your Head**

K-2 "World Record" is	3-5 "World Record" is
70 points.	**125 points.**

Equipment: • Tumbling mats

Activity: The goal of this game is to have as many students as possible in a headstand position simultaneously. All headstands must be unassisted (but spotters may be near). On the signal to begin, the players must do a headstand and hold it for 3 seconds in order for the headstand to be declared legal. One point is awarded for each person successfully holding the headstand during the specified time. Total points are recorded for the record.

Teacher Tip: We review the basic mechanics of a headstand prior to the field day. Students should be given enough space to perform the headstand safely.

3. **Cooperative Get Up**

K-2 "World Record" is	3-5 "World Record" is
80 points.	**118 points.**

Equipment: • None

Activity: The goal of this game is to have as many players as possible go from a sitting to a standing position using a partner's back for support. Players begin sitting down, back to back with elbows interlocked and legs out straight. On the signal to begin, the players have 5 seconds to stand up without releasing their partners. One point is awarded for each pair who stands within the time limit. Total number of successful pairs will be recorded for the record.

Extra Challenge: If time permits, have one-fourth of the class link hands in a circle and try to get up. If successful, do more players. Can you get the entire class to do this?

4.   **Continuous Basketball Dribbles**

Equipment: • Basketballs

K-2 "World Record" is	3-5 "World Record" is
12,300 points.	**21,600 points.**

Activity: The goal of this game is to dribble a basketball as many times as possible. In groups of three, one person will dribble a basketball for 100 dribbles while a partner counts the dribbles. At the end of 100 dribbles, the counter runs to one of the parents who is managing the station. The parent places a mark on a tally sheet.

The dribbler now becomes the counter for the third player. Once the third player finishes 100 dribbles, the ball is given to the original counter. This continues until time is up. The marks on the tally sheet are added together for the class score. If a player loses control of the ball, control must be regained before the counting can continue.

5.   **All Aboard**

K-2 "World Record" is	3-5 "World Record" is
135 points.	**124 points.**

Equipment: • 1 hula hoop

Activity: The goal of this game is to get as many players as possible inside a hoop. To be considered inside the hoop, the player must have at least one body part touching inside the hoop. One point is scored for each person. Players cannot be touching the ground outside the hoop. Players must be able to hold the position for at least 1 second. For an added challenge, decrease the size of the hoop or use a carpet square!

6.   **The Long, Long, Long Jump**

K-2 "World Record" is **870 feet.**	3-5 "World Record" is **1,040 feet.**

Equipment: • Tape measure and cones

Activity: Each student will take a short running start and perform a broad jump. The legal take off point is the same point at which the previous player landed. Use a cone as a marker. Total footage for all participants will be recorded as the record. This is a good station to combine with a water break (half jumping, half getting water).

7.   **Distance Throwing**

K-2 "World Record" is **2,500 points.**	3-5 "World Record" is **3,200 points.**

Equipment: • Cones to mark the distances: 10', 15', 20', 25', 30', 35', 40', 50', 60', 70', etc.
• Softballs (bean bags for primary grades)

Activity: Partners start at a distance of 10 feet apart as marked by the cones and throw a softball to one another using an overhand throw. Only those throws which are done using proper form and are caught by the partner count as successful throws. Once three successful throws are completed by <u>each</u> partner, the student standing on the 10' line moves back to the next cone. Points are earned for the longest successful distance the partners are able to throw. For example, if a pair was able to complete three successful throws at the 60' cones, then 60 points would be earned.

8.   Feet It to Beat It

K-2 "World Record" is	3-5 "World Record" is
9,600 points.	**14,400 points.**

Equipment: • Jump ropes

Activity: In groups of three, one person has the jump rope and will begin jumping, trying to complete 100 jumps. Another player is the counter.   If the jumper gets tired, the third player can take over while the first jumper rests. Once 100 jumps have been completed, the counter runs to one of the parents who is managing the station. The parent places a mark on a tally sheet. It is now time for the counter to jump. One of the other players becomes the new counter. This contines until time is up. The marks on the tally sheet are added together for the class score.

9.   Beanbag Balancing

K-2 "World Record" is	3-5 "World Record" is
10,200 feet.	**14,600 feet.**

Equipment: •   3 beanbags
•   6 cones
•   Popsicle sticks

Activity: Divide the group into three lines. On the signal to begin, the first person in each line begins walking to a cone 50 feet away and back again with a beanbag on his head. On returning, the player gives the beanbag to another player in line who repeats the procedure. If the beanbag falls off his head, the player cannot continue walking until the beanbag is again balanced on his head. Each child is given a popsicle stick every time he returns to the starting line. The total feet for the afternoon will be recorded for the record (multiply the number of sticks by 100 feet).

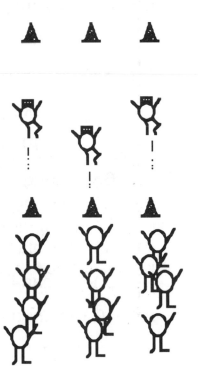

10. The School Song

K-2 "World Record" is	3-5 "World Record" is
120 points	**130 points.**

Equipment: • None

Activivity: The goal of this game is to sing a song as many times as possible. On the signal to begin, one half of the class sings the school song over and over for a 3-minute period. One point is awarded for each time the song is completed. The other half of the class can get water. Now the other half of the class will sing for 3 minutes. Add the two scores together for a class score.

Sample Classroom Scorecard: Here is a copy of a classroom scorecard. This scorecard is taken to the scorer's table at the end of each rotation.

Classroom Teacher's Name: _____

Event: **Score:**

1.)   Pharaoh's Revenge   _____

2.)   That's Using Your Head   _____

3.)   Cooperative Get Up   _____

4.)   Basketball Dribble   _____

5.)   All Aboard   _____

6.)   Long, Long Jump   _____

7.)   Distance Throwing   _____

8.)   Feet It to Beat It   _____

9.)   Bean Bag Balance   _____

10.) School Song   _____

Think Tank Field Day

"Think Tank" Field Day

Background: During this field day, each grade level rotates among six stations. Each of the **six stations** is designated by a color. Rather than use parent volunteers, we use our classroom teacher assistants to lead the six color stations. The classroom teachers stay with their students to help to supervise the students in their grade level. For example, the three kindergarten teachers and their students participate together. Each of the six color stations are designed to have age-appropriate activities. At some color stations, each grade level will have their own different activities. At some stations, all of the students will do the same activity.

Sample Teacher Note: Let's begin with the sample note we gave to our teachers several weeks before the field day.

Dear Teachers:

The "Think Tank" Field Day is coming! Like last year, a teaching assistant will lead each of the stations, introducing the activities and monitoring the progress. The role of every teacher is to assist in seeing that the activity runs smoothly. Feel free to join in the activity.

We will be using a group problem-solving approach. I feel it truly brings together all of what we are trying to accomplish at Orchard School.

Ask the students questions - "How did your group decide that?," "What made you think of that?," perhaps even talking about the successes and failures encountered during the activities. Be the lead cheerleaders! Help the students to encourage each other! You are the catalyst to the learning!

Dedication: I would like to dedicate our field day to Ambrose Brazelton. He is one of the most beautiful, caring, understanding, and generous human beings I have ever met. It would be hard to find someone who cares more for kids and their total education than "Braz."

A Magic Formula for Learning

A Magic Formula for Learning,
Employed with dedication;
Is guaranteed to prod each child
Into rapid education.

Involvement is first!
They cannot learn by merely watching and hearing.
They must touch it, smell it, and taste it too;
Research, intense and searing.

Success is a must!
It stimulates, excites the hunger for more.
Personal wins supported by praise
Inspire the yearn to explore.

But success while doing the same old thing
Is boring, monotonous, a drag.
A Challenge or two deftly presented
Erases the nonchalant bag.

Involvement, Success, and Challenge,
Though important as can be,
Are fruitless without that ingredient
Labeled prescriptive Relevancy.

So, . . . no matter what the subject,
The student's age or size.
This formula makes the learner and learning
Melodiously harmonize.

- Ambrose E. Brazelton -

"Think Tank" Field Day

Schedule of Events: Our field day starts at 9:00 in the morning. Each station is scheduled for 25 minutes. In the afternoon, we have our traditional "Blue and Gold" relays. These are exciting classroom relay races that vary from year to year. We end our field day with popsicles and quiet time.

Field Day Colors: Ask the students to wear your school's colors (our school colors are blue and gold). Remind them to bring water bottles, hats, and sun block. Classes will be called down at 8:50 AM for opening ceremonies. Reminders:

- Please do not leave a station until the signal is given.
- A snack break will be provided. Snacks and drinks will be brought to you at the appropriate time.
- The Blue and Gold Relays will begin at 1:00.
- Popsicles will be served at the end of the relays.

Rotation Guide: Listed below is a rotation schedule and an overview of the day.

	Black	Brown	Red	Orange	Purple	Green
9:00 - 9:25	1st	2nd	5th	4th	3rd	K
9:25 - 9:50	K	1st	2nd	5th	4th	3rd
9:50 - 10:15	3rd	K	1st	2nd	5th	4th
10:15-10:30	------------------ SNACK BREAK -----------------------					
10:30-10:55	4th	3rd	K	1st	2nd	5th
10:55-11:20	5th	4th	3rd	K	1st	2nd
11:20-11:45	2nd	5th	4th	3rd	K	1st
11:45-12:45	------------------ LUNCH BREAK -----------------------					
1:00- 2:30	---------- ORCHARD BLUE AND GOLD RELAYS -------					
2:30- 2:45	------------ POPSICLES AND QUIET TIME --------------					

Green Station Activities: "All for One and One for All"

Background: At the Green Station, the K-2 and 3-5 students have different activities. We'll start with our two K-2 challenges.

1. **Stepping Stones (Grades K-2)**

   Equipment:
   - Carpet squares or pieces of cardboard for each player
   - Ropes to mark the "raging river"

   Activity: Students are placed in groups of 5-6. Each group is given one stepping stone per person. The object is to cross the raging river without falling in (touching the ground) and being swept away. Luckily, each group has a supply of stepping stones that defy the river's swift running current and they even float! Alas, each stepping stone can support no more than two feet at a time.

   Variations:
   1) Provide fewer stones or provide more stones.
   2) Widen the river (flash flood!).
   3) Allow only one foot on each stepping stone.
   4) All stones must be picked up as the group crosses.

2. **Indiana Jones and the Rotating Ropes of Rwanda (Grades K-2)**

   Equipment:
   - Long ropes
   - Panel mats
   - Cones

   Activity: Dr. Jones is at it again! The lost city of Guunsbato, located in the country of Rwanda, is said to contain a very magical elixir! According to legend, whoever drinks from the fountain remains forever young! Guarding this fountain is a myriad of mysterious turning vines (ropes) that twist and wrap around any adventurer who dares to approach.

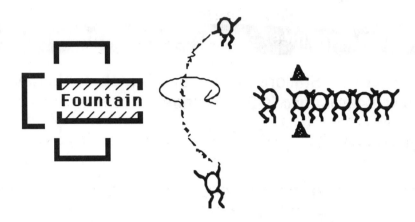

Variations:

1.) Start with one or two turning ropes and add more as the group becomes successful.

2.) First time through - run!

3.) Second time - each adventurer must jump once.

4.) The group must run through in 2's, 4's, 6's, etc.

5.) Count how many adventurers run through successfully before someone is tangled.

3.   A Tie Wins (Grades 3-5)

Equipment:
- Task cards
- Hula hoops
- Cones
- Assorted equipment, balls, etc.

Activity: The goal of this activity is to have the students work and communicate together to produce an active and simultaneous movement "answer" to each of the proposed challenges. Divide the grade levels into groups of 5-6. Give each group a task card to start. When the task has been completed, have the group send one player to get a new task card.

Task Cards

#1

Can your group travel together from one line to the opposite line leaving at the same time and crossing the opposite at exactly the same time?

#2

Can your group drop the hula hoops at the same time to produce one sound?

#3

Can each of your group members throw a ball so all of the balls hit the target at exactly the same time?

#4

Can your group perform 5 curl ups at exactly the same time?

#5

Can your group members, starting with a ball each, toss and catch at exactly the same time?

#6

Can your group perform 25 connected straddle jumps?

#7

Can your group jump rope at the same time?

#8

Can your group stand up at the same time while all holding onto the bike tire?

#9

Can your group members each dribble a ball at exactly the same time?

#10

How many hula-hoops can your group spin at the same time?

Black Station Activities: "Think About This!"

Background: At the Black Station, the K-2 and 3-5 students have different activities. We'll start with our K-2 tag games.

1. **Cooperative Tag Games (Grades K-2)**

    Equipment: • Hula hoops
    • Cones

    Activity #1: Students are placed in groups of 5-6. Each group is given a hoop. The hoop is the life raft onto which all the group members must hold. On the signal to start, the boats begin to travel to the opposite side of the playing area. When "Shark Attack!" is called out the players stop their boats and climb inside. All of the players must be inside their hoops before a count of 10. Anyone on the outside must swim over to the first aid station for some medical treatment (five straddle jumps) and then may rejoin the group.

    Variations: 1.) Give a point for every group member who reaches the opposite side safely. If a group member is left off the life raft, he must remain at the first aid station until his group reaches the opposite side of the playing area. The wounded player may then rejoin his group. 2.) A player left off the life raft must remain at the first aid station until his group can safely arrive for a pick up.

    Activity #2: In the world of "happy-go-lucky" clams, no one is safe. Three or four nuclear reactors (taggers) have had a serious meltdown. If a clam (other players) is tagged by a nuclear reactor, he becomes too weak to go on and slowly begins to lose life. In order to be saved, two other "happy clams" must join hands around the tagged clam and, while jumping up and down, yell "Clam be free! Clam be free! Clam be free!" This gives the tagged clam back all his strength and he may rejoin the game. Clams may not be tagged while freeing other clams.

2. **Bionic Jumping Frogs (Grades 3-5)**

Equipment:
- Playground balls
- Beanbag frogs

Activity: Divide the grade level into groups of 2-3. Each group will have a ball and a beanbag frog. The object is to make the frog "jump" as far as possible by placing the frog on the playground ball and dropping the ball to the floor. When the ball hits the floor, the beanbag frog will bounce from the ball high into the air! The pairs receive 5 minutes of strategy time and 10 minutes of practice time. After the practice time all the groups come together for a "jump off."

Variations: 1.) Count the longest jump of each frog. 2.) Add up the total distance of three jumps. 3.) Have an "all frog" jump, with all of the frogs jumping at the same time.

Orange Station Activities: "Teamwork Counts"

Background: At the Orange Station, the K-2 and 3-5 students have different activities. We'll start with our K-2 cooperative challenges.

1. **Tire Balance (Grades K-2)**

Equipment:
- Two or more car tires

Activity: Divide the grade level into two or more groups so that everyone is at a tire. The object is to get the whole group to balance on a tire for 10 seconds without anyone falling off. Give each group a strategy time before allowing them to start. If successful, combine groups so more people are at the tires. The 10 seconds must be counted by the station leader.

Variations: Here are a few variations to explore -

1.) Climb aboard the tire so that each student is facing out.

2.) Balance only using your right foot, left knee, etc.

3.) Balance using two body parts, then use two different body parts.

2. Earth Orbit (Grades 3-5)

Equipment: • Medicine Ball or large rubber ball

Activity: Students attempt to make the "earth orbit the sun." The earth may not touch the ground. Students roll the earth by lying down on their backs (or sitting) and, using their hands, move the ball along a line of people.

Variations:

1.) Start with a straight line orbit - students sit in a single-file line and pass the ball overhead. This can also be done by having the students sit shoulder to shoulder and pass the ball across their laps.

2.) Increase the area or length of the orbit making the students move to the opposite end to help reach the final destination.

3.) Create different orbit patterns (circle, square, etc.).

4.) How long does it take the earth to orbit? Can it be done faster?

Purple Station Activity: "Adventure Journeys"

Background: At the Purple Station, the K-2 and 3-5 students all perform the same three adventures.

1.   Alaskan Ididarod (Grades K-5)

Equipment: • Scooters
• Jump ropes
• Assorted equipment (mats, cones, etc.)

Activity: An epidemic has just engulfed an isolated Alaskan wilderness town during the worst snow storm of the century. It is up to the town's people to travel via dog sled to neighboring villages to collect medicine to battle the epidemic. Divide the grade level into groups of 5-6. Each group must build a dog sled using the equipment available (three scooters, mats, one long jump rope, etc.). The sled team travels across the frozen tundra to collect medicine for their town. If a sled overturns, the team must return to their own town for repairs.

2. The Great Flood of '99 (Grades K-5)

Equipment:
- Scooters
- Jump ropes
- Assorted equipment (mats, cones, rubber chickens, beanbags, hockey sticks, racquets, etc.)

Activity: After many months of steady rain, a flood has swept through the village of Dry Gulch. In the wake of the flood a very dangerous river now flows through the town. Floating in this river are items which are essential for the villagers to continue living.

Divide the grade level into groups of 5-6. Using the materials provided, each group must build a boat. All group members must travel on the boat as each group begins picking up as much debris as possible. If someone touches the river, he must "swim" to "The Island of Stranded People." That player's group must immediately go to the island to pick up their stranded comrade. While rescuing a stranded player, the group may not pick up any debris.

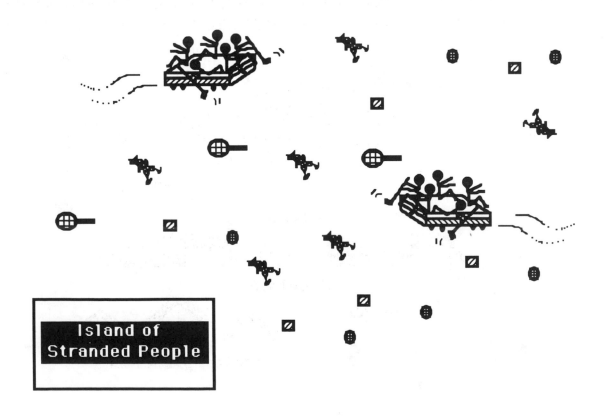

Island of
Stranded People

3. **The Lenape Indian Migration (Grades K-5)**

Equipment:
- Folding mats and incline mats
- Sturdy tables
- A plastic garbage bag per tribe
- One scooter per tribe
- One rope per tribe
- Cones

Activity: Divide the grade level in half. Each group represents a tribe of Lenape Indians. Summer is over. As the winter starts to set in, the Lenape Indians must move to a warmer climate where the water is clean and the food plentiful. There are many perils along the trail - a river to cross and mountains to climb.

To begin the journey, each tribe is equipped with a mat, a large plastic garbage bag, a scooter, and a rope. The river is so fast and so deep, should a tribe member touch it, he would be swept away. The mountains are so high and so steep, should a tribe member fall, he would never be rescued. Upon journey's end each tribe must set up a shelter to protect against the harsh winter winds and blinding snow.

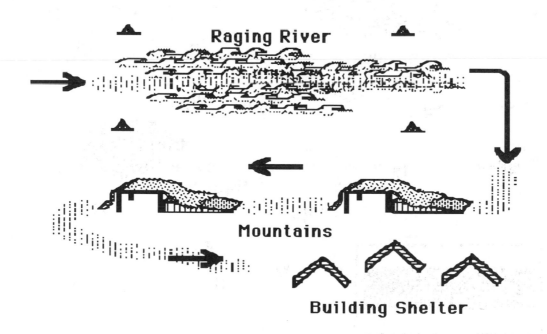

Raging River

Mountains

Building Shelter

Background: At the Brown Station, the K-2 and 3-5 students all perform the same obstacle course. Design it to accommodate several students at a time.

1. **Night Time Jungle Journey (Grades K-5)**

    Equipment:
    - Obstacle course spread out in a designated area
    - Sunglasses ("night vision goggles")
    - Assorted "valuables" (tennis balls, golf balls, etc.)

    Activity: A wild band of monkeys, out looking for a good time, have run off with some very valuable items. Night has come and with it a new moon. Consequently it is very, very dark. Set up in partner groups. One person from each group must travel into the dense jungle to retrieve one of the stolen items. Unable to see because of the darkness, the player is unaware of the perils that await within the boundaries of the jungle.

    However, the partner who is staying behind to protect the other valuables is equipped with a pair of night vision goggles. It is up to him to guide the jungle-goer to an item, helping him to avoid any of the perils. If a player touches one of the obstacles (hurdles, etc.), he must return to the beginning and switch jobs. You may want to set a time limit and change the location of the valuables.

    Options: It is also possible to modify this activity by allowing the older students the choice to wear a blindfold as they are guided through the obstacle course by their partner.

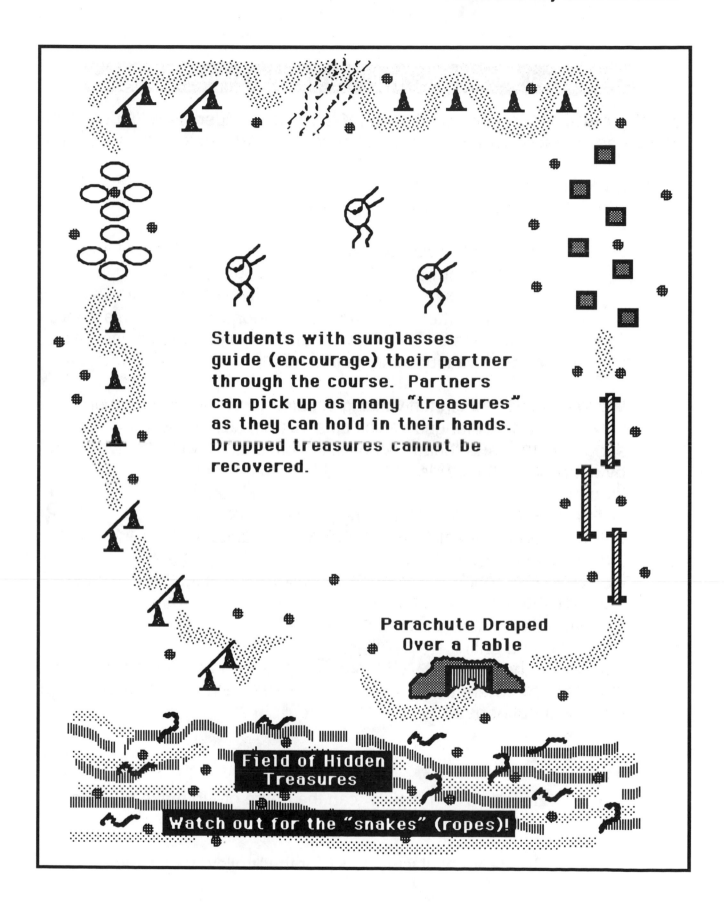

Students with sunglasses guide (encourage) their partner through the course. Partners can pick up as many "treasures" as they can hold in their hands. Dropped treasures cannot be recovered.

Parachute Draped Over a Table

Field of Hidden Treasures

Watch out for the "snakes" (ropes)!

Red Station Activity: "There is no 'I' in Team"

Background: At the Red Station, the K-2 and 3-5 students will perform different tasks. Let's start with the K-2 game!

1. **Balloon Trolley (Grades K-2)**

   Equipment: • Balloons
   • Hula hoops
   • Stopwatch

   Activity: Students attempt to transport balloons from one hula hoop to another one. The balloons are carried between the students (stomachs and backs) without using their hands.

   Warm-up: Students start walking in pairs - one behind the other. Next they are challenged to pick up a balloon using only specific body parts (heads, elbows, knees, etc.). Finish the warm-up by challenging the students to stand front to back and hold a balloon between them. Students may turn in a circle, move from a stand to a squat to a sitting position or balance on one foot - all while holding the balloons (no hands).

   Activity: Challenge the students to walk (or jog, skip, etc. . .) keeping the balloons between the two of them and off the ground until they reach the designated hoops where they drop their balloons.

   Variations:

   1.) How long of a "trolley" can the entire group make (4's, 8's, 16's,. . . entire class)?

   2.) Create an obstacle course for the "trolley" to complete.

2. Radioactive Cylinder Transport (Grades 3-5)

Equipment:
- 2-liter bottles
- Homemade "container handling devices" - made from cutting a plastic milk jug and attaching ropes

Activity: The leaders of this world have officially recognized the hazards of radioactive by-products and have initiated clean-up operations in every country on the planet! The clean-up efforts have been sensational! In fact, the only radioactive waste remaining on Earth has been contained in small cylinders about the size of a 2-liter bottle and it is located here at school!

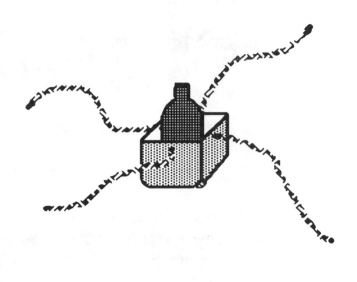

Four students at a time will use the CHD's (container handling devices) to safely transport the containers to an "evaporation site" that will vaporize the toxic waste. Human contact with the container would cause a severe chemical reaction that would set back the clean-up efforts 20 to 30 years. Each student holds a rope as the containers are moved to the evaporation site.

Variations:

1.) The containers must be removed within a set time limit or the toxic waste will leak from the containers.

2.) Only non-verbal commands may be used.

Certificate of Honor

Let it be known that the Bearer of this Certificate Did an Outstanding job During Field Day!

_____
Physical Education Teacher

_____
Principal

Great Activities Publishing Company

International Games Field Day

"International Games" Field Day

Background: Want to learn to play 16 different games from around the world? In this field day, we have designed **16 stations**. Each station is directed by a parent volunteer. The students are divided into 16 groups, each with a teacher or teacher assistant. We rotate groups every **10 minutes** or so.

The theme of this field day is "international." Each activity reflects a country's culture. The following quotes are just thoughts to think about when planning your field day:

"Here is one of life's greatest rules. You cannot hold a torch to light
another's path without brightening your own."
Unknown

"You cannot teach a man anything. You can only help
him discover it within himself."
Galileo

"I cannot teach you anything. I can only provide you with
opportunities to learn."
Unknown

"The experience is over for now, but I have learned.
I know it can happen.
I reach out for tomorrow, ready, excited, open . . .
Today has changed my life.
I have grown."
George Betts

"A mind once stretched by a new idea, never regains its
original dimension."
Unknown

1.   **Chicken Fight (Spain)**

   Equipment: • Flag football belts or scarves - one per student

   Skill Theme: • Balancing
   • Dodging

   Playing Area: Circle (approximately 8-10 feet in diameter)

   Activity: This is a one-on-one game. Each player tucks a flag into his belt. The two players enter the ring at the same time by hopping on the right foot and with the right arm held across the chest. Each player tries to grab the other's flag. A point is scored by a player if he is able to grab his opponent's flag. A point is also scored by a player if his opponent unbends the right arm, touches the ground with the left foot, or leaves the ring.

   Set-up at least three circles.

2.   **King Caesar (Italy)**

   Equipment: • Paper crown (optional)

   Skill Theme: • Chasing
   • Fleeing
   • Dodging

   Playing Area: Open area with circles large enough to allow 3-4 players to stand in them safely.

   Activity: Divide the players into teams of five or more. One player is chosen as "King Caesar," the tagger. The rest of the players stand in one of the circles, a safe area. When King Caesar yells "All out!," all the players attempt to run to a different safe area without being tagged by King Caesar. If tagged, the player joins King Caesar as a tagger.

3.   **Kabaddi (India)**

    Equipment: • None

    Skill Theme: • Chasing
                  • Fleeing
                  • Dodging

    Playing Area: A basketball court works great. Or use an open area, divided by a center line, with marked boundaries.

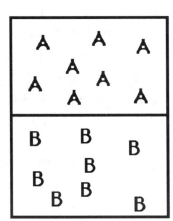

    Activity: Divide the students into two groups. Each group lines up approximately 20 feet from the center dividing line. On the signal to begin, one player from a group runs into the opponents' territory, trying to tag as many players as possible, all the while yelling, "Kabaddi, Kabaddi, Kabaddi, Kabaddi..." without taking a breath!

The player is safe as long as he is yelling "Kabaddi" without taking a breath. If the player stops shouting "Kabaddi" and takes a breath, he may be tagged by the opposing team. If tagged before returning to his own side, he joins the opposing group. All players who are tagged join the opposing group. Group B then sends a player into group A's territory. Kabaddi is pronounced "kuh-BAH-dee".

4.   **Tiger's Ball (Israel)**

    Equipment: • Small balls

    Skill Theme: • Throwing
                  • Catching

    Playing Area: Open space

Activity: There are four or more players for this activity. The players form a circle. One player stands inside the circle. This player is the "tiger." The object is to pass the ball across and around the circle. The player inside the circle tries to intercept the ball. When the tiger intercepts the ball, a new tiger is chosen.

If played with two groups, a player from the opposing group is in the middle of each circle. The first "tiger" to intercept the ball gains a point for his group. A new "tiger" is then placed in each circle. This game is sometimes called "Monkey-in-the-middle" or "Bull in the Ring."

5. **Leg Relay (Israel)**

    Equipment: • Chairs
                    • Small balls

    Skill Theme: • Balancing

    Playing Area: Chairs placed in a single line or in a circle.

    Activity: There are four or more players for this activity. The players sit in the chairs with their legs held out straight in front of them. A ball is placed between the ankles of a starting player. The object is to pass the ball along the line (or circle) using only the legs.

    If the ball is dropped, it goes back to the beginning (choose a new starting player). This could be played as a relay with 10 or more players divided into groups.

6.   **Football (Great Britain)**

     Equipment: • Soccer balls

     Skill Theme: • Catching

     Playing Area: Open area with two lines drawn about 6-8 feet apart.

     Activity: The players form two groups, with each group standing on a line facing each other with their legs spread apart. The ball is rolled down the middle between the two groups. The object is to strike the ball with an open hand so that it goes between the legs of the opposing group. A point is scored every time the ball travels between the legs and across the opposing team's line. Students use good catching skills to prevent this from happening.

     This game may be played with a large group or as few as two (1 versus 1). With more players longer lines are needed. Consider using more than two groups with large numbers (triangle, square formations). One or more balls may be used with larger groups.

7.   **Old Mrs. Winter (Czechoslovakia)**

     Equipment: • A red flag tied to a stick (Old Mrs. Winter)

     Skill Theme: • Chasing
                        • Fleeing
                        • Dodging
                        • Throwing
                        • Catching

     Playing Area: Open area with boundaries

     Activity: The players are divided into two groups. One of the groups has the red flag and the opposing team begins as the catchers. The game begins with the two groups lined up facing each other.

140

The catchers step forward and yell:

"We've come to get Old Mrs. Winter. It's time to throw her in the river."

The friends of Old Mrs. Winter pass her from player to player as they run to avoid the catchers. If tagged, the flag is given to the opposing group. Play continues as the friends of Old Mrs. Winter attempt to get her back! This game is called "Keep Away" in the U.S.

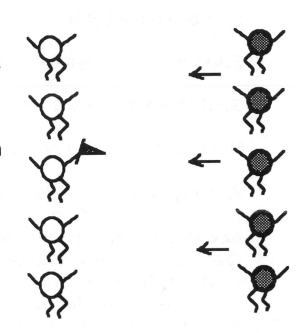

8. **Shadow Tag (Australia)**

Equipment: • None

Skill Theme: • Chasing
• Fleeing
• Dodging

Playing Area: Open area with boundaries

Activity: Players start in a scattered formation. One or more players are designated taggers. The taggers tag by stepping on the shadows of the other players. If tagged, the player becomes a tagger and the tagger becomes a runner. In Japan this game is called "Kage-Bohi-Onigo."

9.	1, 2, 3 Dragon (China)

Equipment:	• None

Skill Theme:	• Chasing
	• Fleeing
	• Dodging

Playing Area: Open area

Activity: The players make a
straight line with one player
behind another. Each player
puts his hands on the shoulders of the player in front.
The beginning of the line is
the dragon's head. The end of
the line is the dragon's tail.
The tail yells, "1,2,3,dragon!" to start the game. The head player attempts to tag the tail without breaking up the line. If anyone lets go,
the dragon dies and the players rotate. If the head tags the tail the
dragon wins and there is much rejoicing!

The players rotate positions if the dragon wins! To rotate positions,
the head and the next player in line break away from the front of the
line and join on the end. Results: a new head and tail!

10.	Presohan (Philippines)

Equipment:	• One can
	• One beanbag per player

Skill Theme:	• Chasing
	• Fleeing
	• Dodging
	• Throwing

Playing Area: Two lines drawn parallel to each other about 20 feet
apart. A circle is drawn in the space between the lines.

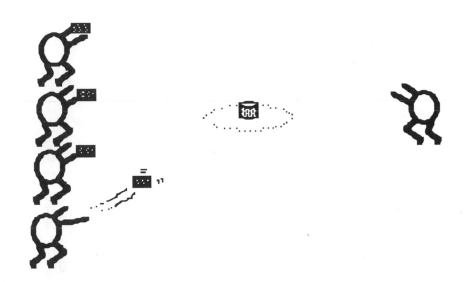

Activity: One player is designated as the tagger or "prisoner." The tagger places the can in the circle and stands behind one of the lines. The other players stand behind the opposite line with each holding a beanbag. One player at a time attempts to hit the tagger's can with his beanbag. If successful, the player must run, retrieve his beanbag, and cross safely back over the line before the tagger can retrieve his can, place it back in the circle and tag the player. If a player misses, he must wait until another player hits the tagger's can. Then both players run to retrieve their beanbags before being chased by the tagger. If a player is tagged, a new tagger is named and the game continues.

Traditionally, this game is played with all players having cans. In our version, we have substituted beanbags for the thrower's cans.

11. **Third Man Out (Denmark)**

   Equipment: • None

   Skill Theme: • Chasing
            • Fleeing
            • Dodging

   Playing Area: Large circle, approximately 20 feet in diameter

Activity: One player is chosen as the tagger. A second player is chosen as the runner. The rest of the players stand with a partner, one behind the other and facing in the same direction.

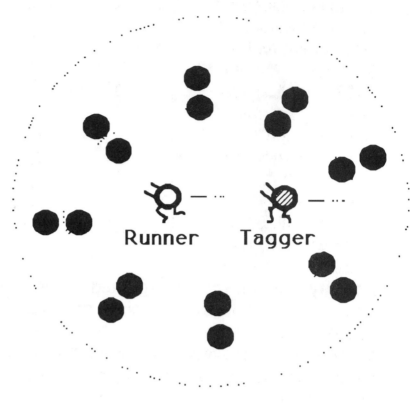

Runner   Tagger

The tagger chases and tries to tag the runner. If tagged, the runner becomes the tagger and the tagger becomes the runner. To be safe, the runner may stop in front of a partner group. When this happens the player in the back becomes the new runner. All players must stay within the circle.

12. **Cheetah, Cheetal (India)**

Equipment: • None

Skill Theme: • Chasing
• Fleeing
• Dodging

Playing Area: Large open area with two lines (5 feet apart) drawn parallel at the center of the playing area and a line drawn at each end of the field.

Activity: Divide the players into two even groups. Each group lines up behind its own line at mid-field, facing the opposing group. One group is designated as the "cheetahs," the other group as the "cheetals." One person stands between the groups at midfield. The leader calls out either "cheetahs" or "cheetals." The group whose name is called becomes the taggers and chases the opposing group back to their line. The team whose name is not called tries to run safely back to their own end line before being tagged by a tagger. Anyone tagged joins the opposing team for the next round.

13. January (Canada)

Equipment: • None

Skill Theme: • Chasing
• Fleeing
• Dodging

Playing Area: Open area with end line

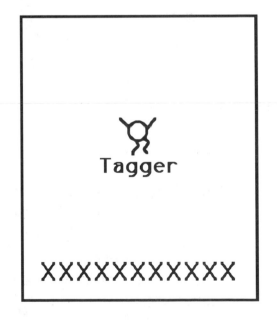

Activity: One player is chosen as the tagger. The tagger stands in the middle of the field. The other players stand behind one of the end lines. One by one the players try to cross the field to the opposite end line without being tagged. If tagged, the players join the original tagger in the middle of the field.

Whenever the tagger(s) chant the rhyme below all the players cross at the same time.

" January, January,
   One, two, three.
   If you don't run now,
   I'll catch you where you be."

When all of the players have been caught, begin another game by selecting a new tagger.

14. Drie Blikkies (South Africa)

Equipment:
- 3 cans
- 1 ball
- 4 bases

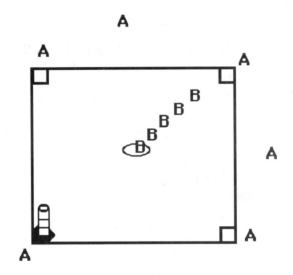

Skill Theme:
- Throwing
- Catching

Playing Area: Open area - a circle (3-foot diameter) surrounded by four bases.

Activity: This game will need two teams. Team A starts as the fielders and Team B as the runners. The fielders place one player at each of the bases. The runners line up at the center circle. The "blikkies" (cans) are stacked on top of each other at the "blikki post" (home base). The first player from Team B throws or rolls the ball, trying to topple the blikkies. Each player takes a turn until the blikkies are toppled.

Once the blikkies are knocked down, the player who knocked them down attempts to run to first base. The Team A player at the "blikki post" catches the ball and throws it to his teammate at the first base.

If the player at the first base catches the ball before the runner makes it there, Team B is out and the two groups switch positions. If the runner makes it to the base before the ball arrives, he is safe and may attempt to run to the next base.

The runners score 1 point for every base reached safely. Once a player attempts to run to the next base there is no going back. If a player is "tagged" out, the two groups switch positions and no points are awarded, regardless of the number of bases reached safely.

Drie Blikkies is pronounced "duh-REE BLICK-ees."

15. **El Reloj (Argentina)**

Equipment: • One long jump rope

Skill Theme: • Jumping

Playing Area: Open area

Activity: Two players are the rope turners, the rest line up as jumpers. The first person jumps the rope once and yells "1 o'clock!" The second player jumps the rope twice and shouts "2 o'clock!" This continues until the group reaches 12 o'clock with a player jumping 12 times. If someone

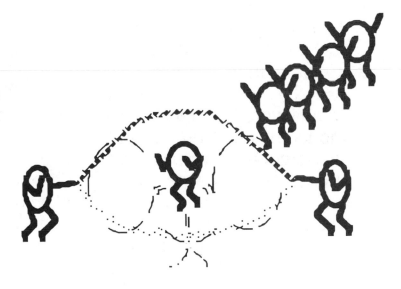

misses, the group starts again at 1 o'clock. El Reloj is pronounced "el REL-lo" which means "the clock."

16. Gathering Stars (Africa - Pygmies of Gabon)

Equipment: • None

Skill Theme: • Chasing
  • Fleeing
  • Dodging

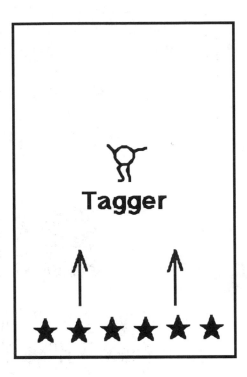

Playing Area: Open area with two end lines

Activity: One player is designated as the "Tagger." It is suggested that there be one catcher for every 10 players to start the game. The rest of the players stand behind one end line.

The tagger(s) chant:

" Star light, star bright,
   How many stars are out tonight?'

The players reply:

"More than you can catch and carry!"

The players then try to cross to the opposite side without being tagged by a catcher. If tagged, the player joins the catchers for the next round. Another alternative is for the player to switch jobs with the catcher.

Note:

1.) In the U.S. and Canada this game is called "Blackberry."

2.) This game is based on a myth. The legend says that the Milky Way is made up of broken stars. The gods go along gathering up the broken stars and putting them into baskets. The stars are used as fuel for the sun to burn.

BINGO
Field Day

"BINGO" Field Day

Background: The BINGO Field Day is based on the game of BINGO. During this field day, the students participate at **24 different activity stations**, trying to complete a "BINGO."

How We Do It: This field day lasts approximately 2 hours with all 600 of our students outside at the same time. It is amazing how well this format works! We have found our students are on their best behavior because they get so involved and want to participate. This field day would also work well if you divided the school into K-2 and 3-5 groups. Your 3-5 students could participate in the morning and K-2 students in the afternoon.

BINGO! Each student is given a "BINGO Card." Please see the samples that are provided. The students are divided by their classroom teacher into **small groups of two or three**. These "buddy groups" are allowed to go to any one of the 24 stations. Each of the stations has been randomly assigned a BINGO number from 1-24. After participating at that station, one of the parent volunteers stamps the student's BINGO Card with a rubber stamp. For example, if the obstacle course station was #22, the parent volunteer would use a rubber stamp to cover the "22" on the student's BINGO Card. Since the students do not know the numbers associated with the stations, they get really excited as they begin to get more and more numbers stamped on their BINGO Cards!

FREE SPACE: The space in the center of our BINGO Cards (Free Space) is our Karaoke station. Our music teacher is in charge of this station. We set-up a huge stage and have 20 or more of the students' favorite sing-along songs. We include old favorites such as "Twinkle, Twinkle, Little Star" and the "Alphabet Song," as well as more up-to-date music.

Awards: When a student gets a BINGO (five squares in a line), they report to the Award Station and get a sports bookmark stapled to their card. They get a bookmark for each BINGO. When a student has all of his squares marked out, he earns a field day certificate. These incentives really help to keep the students involved in all of the stations.

Field Day Poster: We also made a special poster to get our teachers excited about our field day. We used candy bar wrappers to compose the following sign:

Our Field Day is coming up  !

This will be
the best field day,

Our

field day  !

"BINGO FIELD DAY"
coming soon to a school near you!

Other: Since this field day is so dependent on parent volunteers, we have a special raffle for our classroom teachers. For each volunteer the teacher recruits, the teacher fills out a raffle slip and places it in a decorated coffee can in the faculty room. The more volunteers a teacher recruits, the more chances at winning the raffle! The raffle prizes are things we have collected during the year - leftover "Jump Rope for Heart" items, gifts donated by local businesses, etc. We have the raffle during lunch on the day of field day. This system really works for us!

Sample Raffle Tickets

"Game Day": Here's a simple way to set-up the activity stations that has worked quite well for us. We have 25 folding chairs lined up in the gym. Each folding chair has the game directions taped to it and all of the necessary equipment and supplies sitting under it. The parent volunteers assemble in the gym, select a chair (activity station), take everything outside, choose a spot for the activity, direct the game, and bring everything back in after the field day is over.

Field Day Stations: Unlike field days with a theme, you can literally use any of the activity stations found in this book for your BINGO Field Day. For this reason, we did not include descriptions of sample stations for you. All you need are 24 stations and you're ready to go!

BINGO Cards and Bookmarks: You will find samples of four BINGO cards. Please feel free to use these or make your own.

We use the four different BINGO cards printed on several colors of paper. We have found that doing this keeps the kids a little "confused," and many of them think we have printed hundreds of different BINGO cards!

A sheet of the BINGO bookmarks is also included. These can also be printed on different colored paper.

Field Day
BINGO

15	24	3	9	14
7	11	17	20	6
13	8	🎵	2	22
10	4	21	1	19
18	23	12	16	5

Name _____

Field Day
BINGO

10	3	5	22	15
17	16	1	13	6
20	9	🎵	14	12
19	21	8	23	2
4	7	18	11	24

Name _____

Field Day
BINGO

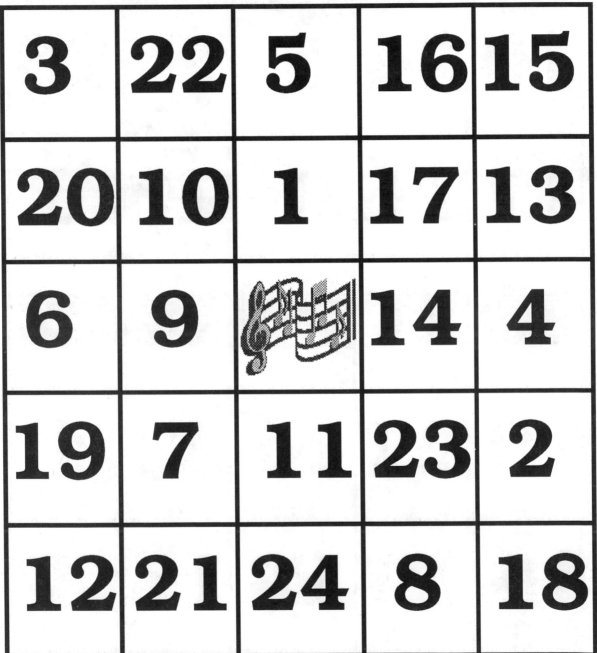

3	22	5	16	15
20	10	1	17	13
6	9	🎵	14	4
19	7	11	23	2
12	21	24	8	18

Name _____

19	24	5	9	23
1	11	17	20	6
13	8	♪	12	22
10	21	15	7	4
18	14	2	16	3

Name _____

BINGO
Field Day

BINGO
Field Day

BINGO
Field Day

BINGO
Field Day

Fit, Healthy, and Ready to Learn Field Day

"Fit, Healthy, and Ready to Learn"

Background: The Washington State Commission on Student Learning has developed "Essential Learnings" for all subject areas for our K-12 students. One of the "Health and Physical Education" standards addresses that students will know and understand the components of physical fitness. These components are a combination of health-related and skill-related items. To help our students understand and apply these physical fitness components, we have designed a "Fit, Healthy, and Ready to Learn" Field Day.

How We Do It: In the spring, we have each of our 4th and 5th grade students design a game or activity using one (or more) of the fitness components. Each student is given this as a homework assignment. The students select one of the fitness components and design a game that could be used on field day.

Selecting the Games: After the homework assignments are completed, the game is evaluated three times: self evaluation, peer evaluation, and teacher evaluation. As a class, we decide which games would be appropriate for field day.

Field Day Format: For our field day, we use **18-24 activity stations**. Parent volunteers are used to supervise and run the events. Sometimes, we have the actual student who has designed the game or activity to help at the station. The field day lasts about 2 hours.

Awards: Each student is given an "Awards Wreath" that is worn around his neck. This is a 2-3 foot length of florist ribbon tied in a circle. Students are allowed to play the games in small groups of 2-3 students. After playing a game, the parent volunteer gives an "award marker" to the student that is stapled to the student's ribbon.

The award marker is a square piece of colored paper with the appropriate fitness component on it. Each classroom teacher carries staplers with them during our field day. The student finds a classroom teacher and the paper is stapled to the ribbon. The kids really enjoy trying to fill their ribbons with the colorful slips of paper!

"Fit, Healthy, and Ready to Learn" Assignment

Name: _____

Classroom Teacher: _____

Health-Related Fitness Components:

- Cardiovascular Endurance   __   (Please check)
- Upper Body Strength/Endurance   __
- Healthy Weight   __
- Abdominal Fitness   __
- Lower Back Flexibility   __

Sport-Related Fitness Components:

- Agility & Reaction Time   __
- Balance   __
- General Sport-Related   __
- Explosive Power   __
- Speed   __

Name of the Game: _____

Equipment Needed: _____
_____

How to Play: _____
_____
_____
_____
_____
_____
_____
_____
_____

(Please use additional sheets if needed. Diagrams are encouraged!)

"Fit, Healthy, and Ready to Learn" Field Day

Sample Activities: Listed below are examples of the activity stations we have for our "Fit, Healthy, and Ready to Learn" Field Day.

1.) Cardiovascular Endurance -

- Pacer Test (Fitnessgram)
- Mile Walk/Run
- Aerobic Dance/Line Dance Routines
- Jump Rope Activities
- Power Walking with Heart Rate Monitors
- Calculating Your Target Heart Rate

2.) Upper Body Strength/Endurance -

- Pull-Up Test
- Push-Up Test (Fitnessgram)
- Parachute Games
- Dyna Bands
- Hand Weights

3.) Healthy Weight -

- Body Mass Index
- Skin Calipers

4.) Abdominal Fitness -

- Curl-ups
- Fitnessgram curl-up assessment
- Leg lifts

5. Lower Back Flexibility -

- Appropriate Stretches (We use the handouts from the book Fit to Try! by Cindy Bross, published by Great Activities)
- Back Saver Sit and Reach Test
- Student Flexibility Profile

6.) **Agility & Reaction Time -**

- Soccer Dribble
- Cup Stacking
- Shuttle Run
- "Gravity Grab" (using the reaction time strips)
- "Red Light, Green Light," "Cranes and Crows"

7.) **Balance -**

- Balance Beam Activities
- Stork Stand/Blindfolded Stork Stand
- Tripods, Headstands, Cartwheels
- Handstand Contest

8.) **General Sport-Related Items -**

- Juggling
- Jump Rope Skills
- Softball Throw for Distance
- Basketball Dribbling Obstacle Course
- Football Accuracy Throw

9.) **Explosive Power -**

- Standing Broad Jump
- Vertical Jump

10.) **Speed -**

- 50-Yard Dash
- Relays

**"Fit, Healthy, and
Ready to Learn!"**

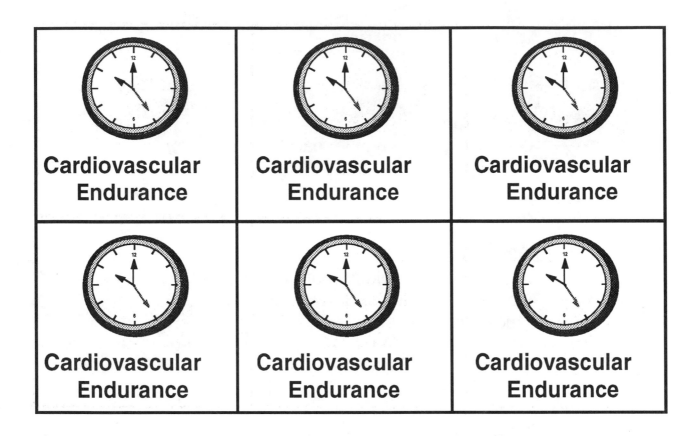

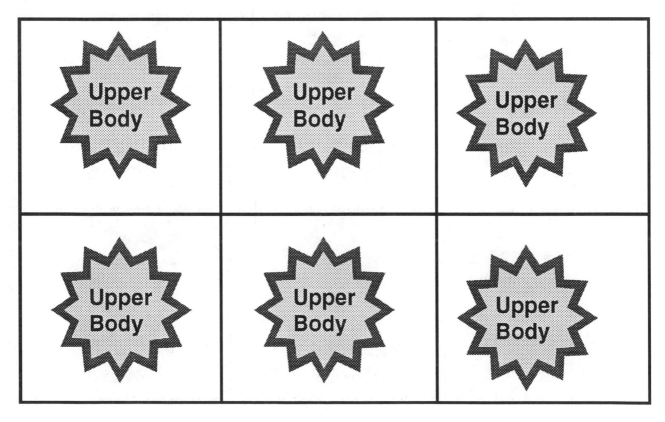

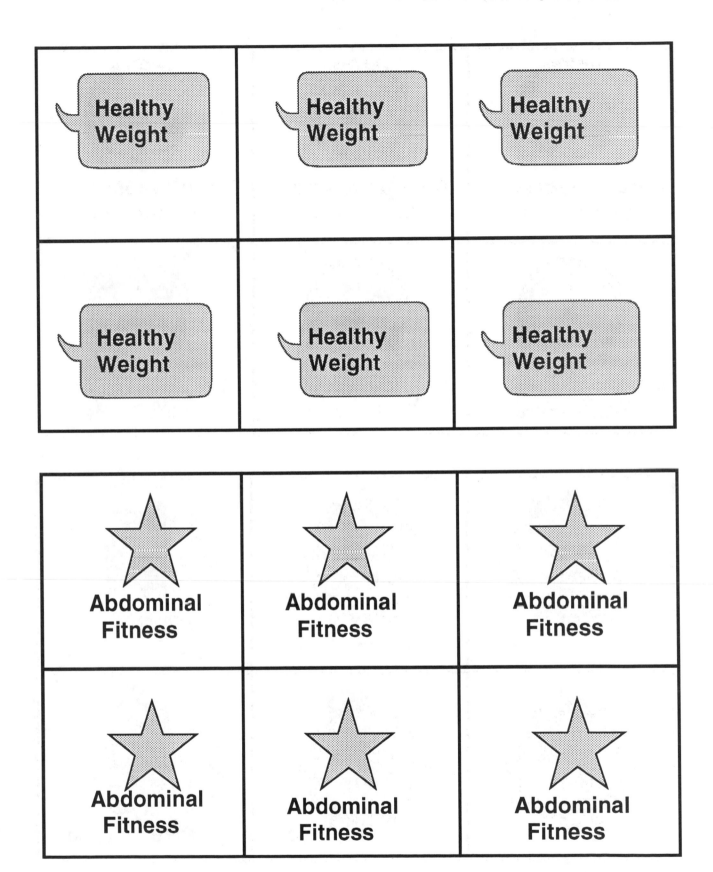

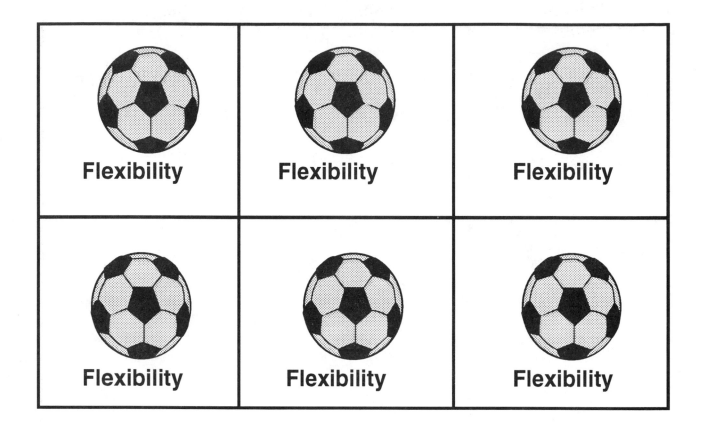

Flexibility	**Flexibility**	**Flexibility**
Flexibility	**Flexibility**	**Flexibility**

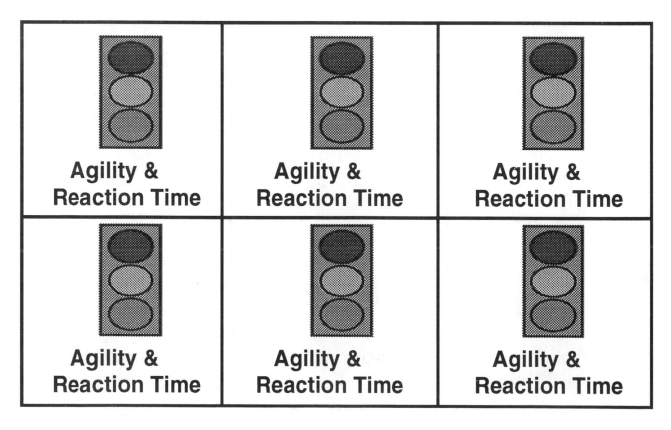

Agility & Reaction Time	**Agility & Reaction Time**	**Agility & Reaction Time**
Agility & Reaction Time	**Agility & Reaction Time**	**Agility & Reaction Time**

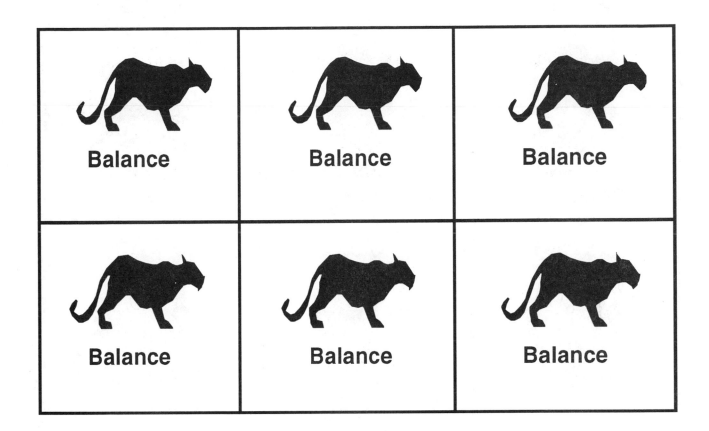

Balance	Balance	Balance
Balance	Balance	Balance

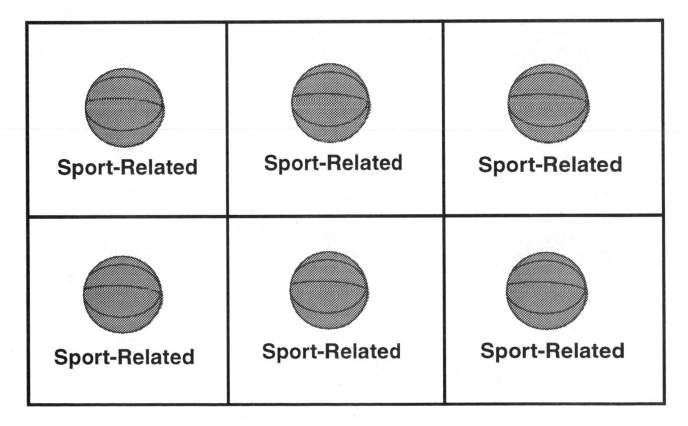

Sport-Related	Sport-Related	Sport-Related
Sport-Related	Sport-Related	Sport-Related

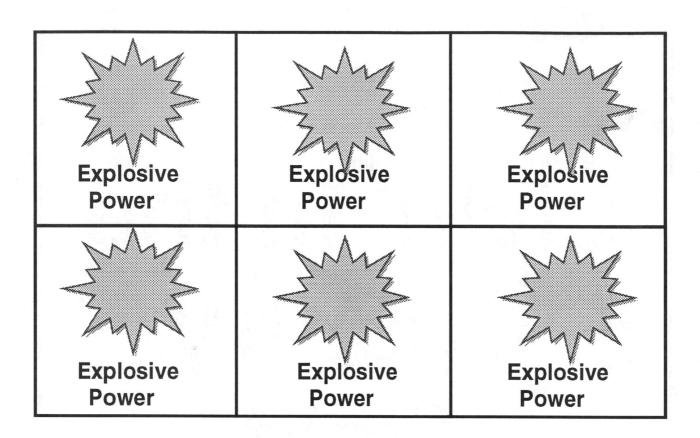

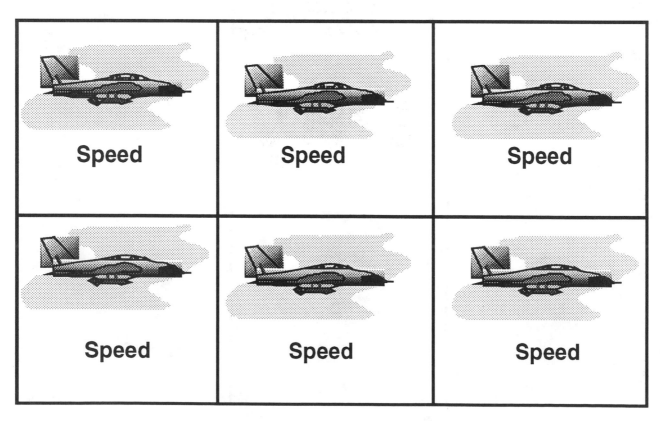

Livin' in the Country Field Day

"Livin' in the Country" Field Day

Background: The theme for this field day is taken from the elementary school musical called "Mouse Country" by James Leisy. Classroom teachers had the music and words for the song, "Livin' in the Country" weeks prior to field day. Students practiced the song during their music classes. While having the music from "Mouse Country" is desirable, you will be able to have a great field day without the song.

How We Did It: Bandanas were made for each student. We were able to make our own bandanas from old bed sheets that our local hospital sold to us at a bargain price. So, the PTA spent $20 on sheets and that supplied enough triangular bandanas for the whole school (600 kids)!

Field Day Format: The "Livin' in the Country" Field Day began with a school assembly. The assembly included the following items:

- A guest country yodeler (one of our own staff members)
- "What do I hear?" "Yee Haw!" (Anytime I yelled that question, the students responded with "Yee Haw!")
- Staff lasso twirling and hog calling contest
- Introduction of the sheriff (principal)
- Entire school singing "Livin' in the Country"

Bandana Stamps: There are **22 stations** in this field day. The field day is "carnival-style," with the **students moving from station to station at their own speed and desire**. After playing a station (run by parent volunteers) the student would receive a rubber stamp on his bandana. Each station had a stamp with a different design and color. At the end of the field day, each student had a colorful bandana to take home! If possible, try to use permanent, fast-drying ink with your stamps. Remind the students not to get the bandanas wet (for example, no ducking your head under the water fountain) or else the ink might smear and get on their clothes.

Memo to Teachers

Subject: "Livin' in the Country" Field Day, June 15th

Field Day is Coming! This is a reminder that there will be no physical education or music classes on field day. During the morning all-school Awards Assembly, Judy (music teacher) and I are having to set up our field day to prepare for our noon meeting with our parent volunteers. We appreciate your understanding.

Pick-up Your Bandanas: Bandanas are available in the faculty room. Please be sure to pick up one for each student. It would be a good idea to write the students' names on them in case they get misplaced. You may also choose to write "Field Day 2001" on them. The bandanas will only be worn "country style" around the neck or carried in the hand. They are not to be worn anywhere else.

Optional Activity: Your class may want to design a ranch "brand" for your class. You may want to draw the "branding mark" on their cheeks with face paint.

Afternoon Festivities: The adult volunteers will help me set up outside from 12:00 - 12:30. All classes will meet outside on the blacktop facing the portable PA system. We will sing "Livin' in the Country" together, give a few basic rule reminders, and then start the field day!

Ending Times: The field day will end at 1:55 for primary grades and 2:20 for intermediate grades.

WARNING!!! "Wanted" posters of staff members will be hidden around the playground area. When a student finds a "wanted" poster, he takes it to the sheriff (our principal) and that person will be put in the "pokey" for a couple of minutes. Don't forget to encourage your students to dress using country western "duds" on Monday. **Thanks!**

"Livin' in the Country" Stations

1. **County Jail**

   Equipment:
   - Wanted posters of staff members
   - Jail (tumbling mats stood up on end)
   - Sheriff/deputies
   - Handcuffs

   Activity: Prior to field day beginning, we hide the "wanted" posters around the playground (see sample poster). If a student finds a poster during field day, he finds that teacher and escorts the teacher to the county jail. The sheriff (principal) puts plastic handcuffs on the teacher. The jail consists of old tumbling mats stood up on end. We make "bars" using gym floor tape on the mats to look like the cell bars. Teachers stay in jail for about 2-5 minutes and then are let free. The fun thing is that the staff doesn't know how many posters we have made of each of them!!!

2. **Boot Hill Target Toss Kickin'**

   Equipment:
   - Two cones
   - Five hula hoops

   Activity: Scatter the hula hoops on the ground. The student stands between the two cones, loosens a shoe, and attempts to kick his shoe into a hula hoop. Be sure to have the line for this game off to the side rather than behind the kicker. Some shoes do tend to fly in the wrong direction (ie. backwards).

John McHenry, Jr.

Last seen in room #21 on the second grade wing.
Wanted for driving an unwashed vehicle.
Approach with caution!

3. Crawdad Fishin'

Equipment:
- Wading pool
- Marbles
- Water
- Towels

Activity: Fill the wading pool with water and add the marbles. Participants take one shoe off and try to pick up one or more marbles with their toes. Have towels handy for drying off the students' feet.

4. Panning for Gold

Equipment:
- Gold nuggets (made from gold spray paint)
- Sand toys (the sifter kind)
- Plastic coins
- A gravel and/or sandy area

Activity: Using gold spray paint, make gold nuggets from small rocks. Spread the gold in a gravel area. We use the gravel under one of the playground toys. Students use the sand toys to sift through the gravel to find the gold nuggets. Some kids prefer to keep the gold nuggets, but most students like trading in five pieces of gold for a plastic coin (from the Oriental Trading Company's catalog).

5. Lasso Twirling

Equipment:
- 8 lassoes

Activity: At this station students are able to practice lasso twirling. We just let the students practice twirling.

6. Tumbling Tumbleweeds

Equipment:
- Cones
- Broken hula hoops
- Soccer balls

Activity: Goals are made by putting the ends of a broken hula hoop into the traffic cones. Students take turns kicking "tumbleweeds" (soccer balls) into the goals.

7.   **Pancake Flipping**

      Equipment: • Badminton racquets
                         • Polyspots

      Activity: The students place a polyspot on the face of the racquet. Toss the polyspot into the air (with a little flip) and attempt to catch it on the racquet.

8.   **Calf Roping**

      Equipment: • Rings
                         • A set of "horns"
                         (chair legs - place a chair on the ground so that the legs are facing the student) or use a rocking horse.

      Activity: We use a child's rocking horse and a set of Olympet rings for this game. Students try to throw the rings onto the horse's head.

9.   **Pony Express**

      Equipment: • Brooms (or stick ponies)
                         • Cones
                         • Manila envelopes

      Activity: Students gallop while riding a "horse" (we found swimming Fun Noodles with horse heads on the ends) around a cone and back. Be sure to have students carry the "important" mail!! Four students can race at a time.

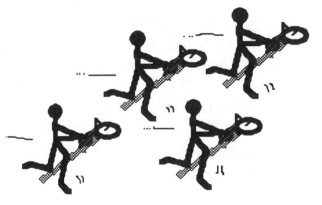

10. Covered Wagon Races

Equipment:
- Scooters
- Folded tumbling mats
- Broken hula hoops
- Butcher paper
- Duct tape

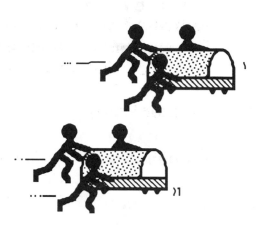

Activity: You'll need to make several "covered wagons" for this activity. A covered wagon is made by placing a folded tumbling mat on two scooter boards. Use duct tape to place broken hula hoops over the top of the mat. Attach butcher paper to the broken hula hoops to finish the covered wagon.

We usually build three covered wagons. Assign 2-3 students per covered wagon and have the students push it through a designated race course. Be sure to have extra duct tape on hand for repairs!!

11. Laundry Day

Equipment:
- Twine/clothesline cord
- Clothespins
- Old clothes
- Big bucket of soapy water
- Bucket of water

Activity: This activity is done as an individual race with 2-3 students. The students pick up an article of clothing off the ground and run forward to a bucket of soapy water. Students must dip the clothes into the soapy water and then continue on to the bucket of water where they rinse the clothes. After rinsing, the students hang the clothes up on the clothesline and return to the starting line. We've also done this as a relay. The next person in line would reverse the order (i.e. take the clothes down, rinse in the water, etc.).

12. Cracker Chew and Whistle

Equipment: • Crackers
• Water and paper cups

Activity: Two to three students at a time compete against each other. The students are given a soda cracker. Who will be the first player to eat the cracker and whistle?

13. Gopher Holes

Equipment: • Coffee cans
• Indoor hockey sticks
• Whiffle balls

Activity: The coffee cans are set up in a miniature golf pattern. We decorate the coffee cans to look like mole holes with beady little eyes inside. Students use the indoor hockey sticks to hit the whiffle balls into the cans.

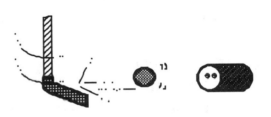

14. Shooting Gallery

Equipment: • Squirt guns
• Whipped cream
• Toy pinwheels
• Tape

Activity: The pinwheels are hung from a piece of outside playground equipment. The game leader squirts whipped cream on the center of the pinwheel and students attempt to clean the whipped cream off by using squirt guns.

15. Hay Hurdles

Equipment: • "Bales of hay" (cardboard boxes)

Activity: We covered the boxes with yellow butcher paper and painted them to look like hay bales. Set the boxes up approximately 8 feet from each other.
We usually set up two straight lines so that two students can race each other. Students run down and back jumping over the hay.

16. Chalk Art

Equipment: • Sidewalk chalk
 • Sidewalks

Activity: Allow students to draw "cowboy" type pictures on the sidewalk or blacktop. Monitor closely so that nothing inappropriate is drawn.

17. Cow Milking

Equipment: • Sponges
 • Buckets
 • Water
 • Stools
 • Cups

Activity: Set up two milking stations so that students can race against each other. Students run to the stools and sit down. They pick up the sponge, soak it in the water bucket, and squeeze the water into a cup. When the cup is full, they carry it back to the starting line.

18. Cattle Round-up

Equipment: • Hockey sticks
• Whiffle balls

Activity: Two or more students can participate at a time. Scatter yellow and red whiffle balls out on the ground. On the signal to begin, the player with the yellow hockey stick attempts to gather all of the yellow whiffle balls into one area while the red player does the same thing. The first player to gather all of his whiffle balls wins.

19. Horseshoes

Equipment: • Rubber horse-shoes
• Stakes

Activity: Give each student three tries to ring a horseshoe on the stake. Always remember safety. Clearly mark the area so that students do not walk through the middle of the horseshoe game. We have found that it works well to put the stake near a softball backstop.

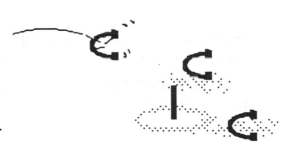

20. Hog Calling

Sou-ee!

Equipment: • Karaoke machine
• Extension cord

Activity: Allow students to try their hand at hog calling using the microphone from a karaoke machine.

21. Corn Chucking

Equipment:
- Corn cobs
- Cones
- Mats

Activity: Place cones in a straight line (or use a measuring tape) to mark distance. Students lay down on their backs (on the mat) and grasp a corn cob between their feet. Students attempt to throw the corn cob as far as possible by quickly bringing their legs overhead.

50'

40'

30'

20'

10'

22. River Jumping

Equipment:
- Tumbling mats

Activity: Use vinyl floor tape to mark fish, alligators, etc. on the mats. Students can get a running start and attempt to jump over the mats.

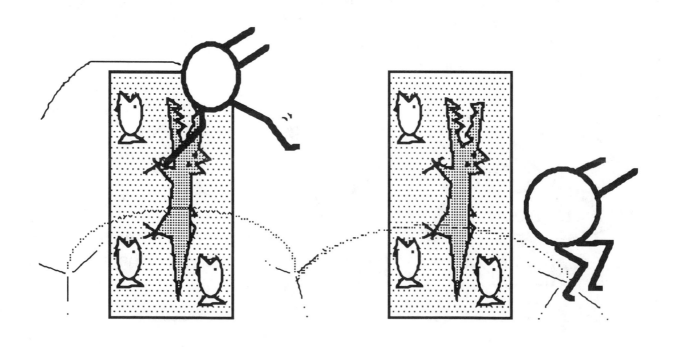

Olympics
Field
Day

"Olympics" Field Day

Background: Our "Olympics" Field Day is designed to take place in one afternoon (approximately 2 hours) for a total of 600 students at one time. The **activities are "carnival-style"** on our two playfields and the blacktop area. This allows the individual students to visit any of the **22 stations** during the field day.

Medal Medallions: Prior to our Opening Ceremony, the students are given medals to wear around their necks. These medals are made from the lids of frozen juice concentrate and florist ribbon. In addition, each classroom designs and decorates a class banner to be carried during the procession.

Opening Ceremonies: Our Opening Ceremony consists of the following -

- Procession of athletes to the blacktop area
- Welcome by principal
- Star Spangled Banner
- Recognition of participating classes (showing their banners)
- Introduction of our special guest speaker
- Olympic Oath led by our guest speaker
- Running of the torch (5th grade relay with a fake torch)
- "Let the Games begin!"

Field Day Format: The students play the station games at their own pace. At each game, the students have the possibility of winning a Gold Medal, Silver Medal, or Bronze Medal. The game medals are printed on different colored paper and cut into squares. Each game supervisor (volunteer parent) has three envelopes containing each of the medals. The classroom teachers walk around the field day area carrying staplers.

Awarding the Medals: After playing the game, the student finds a teacher with a stapler. The teacher staples the paper medal onto the student's ribbon. Students attempt to fill up their ribbons with medals. The end of field day is signaled with "Olympic Spirit" music played over the loudspeaker. This tells students that it is time to find their teacher and return to class.

Gold Medals

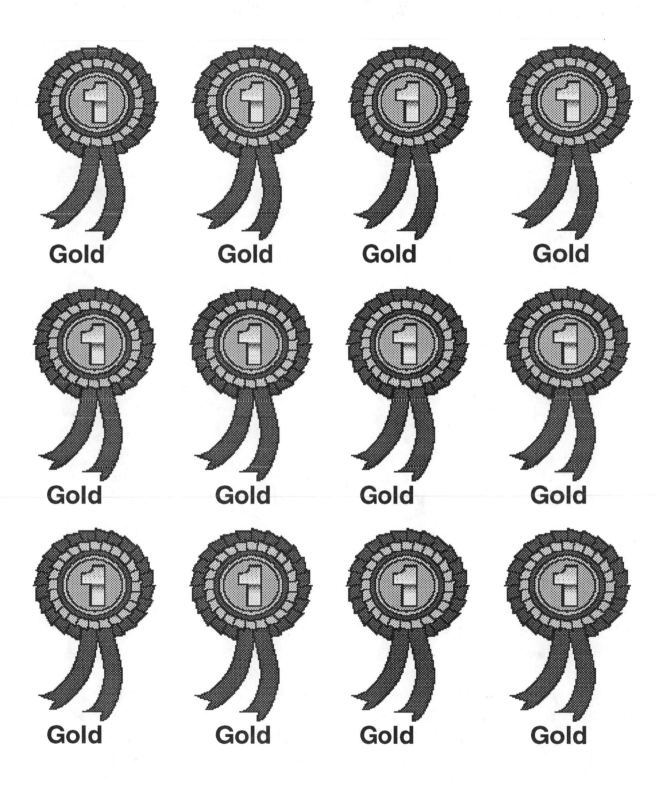

Silver Medals

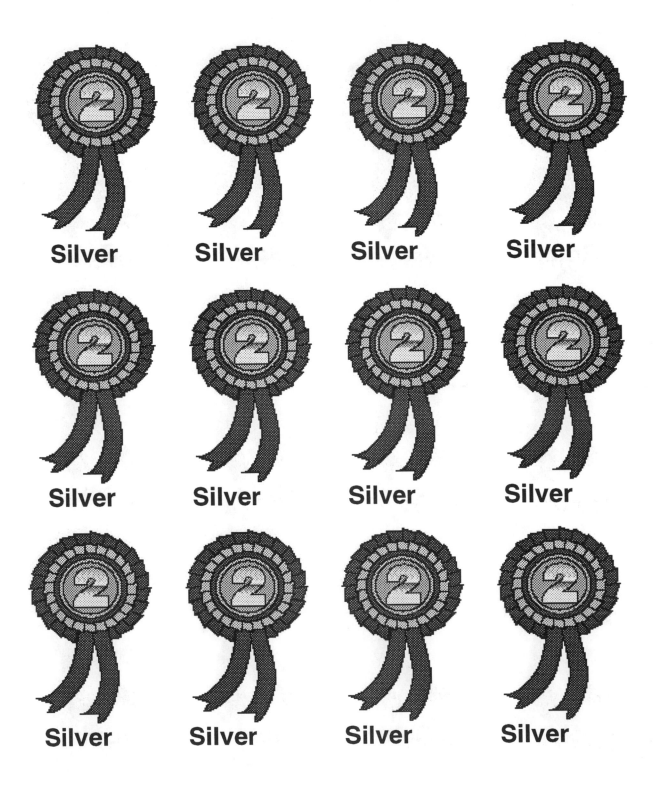

Silver Silver Silver Silver

Silver Silver Silver Silver

Silver Silver Silver Silver

Bronze Medals

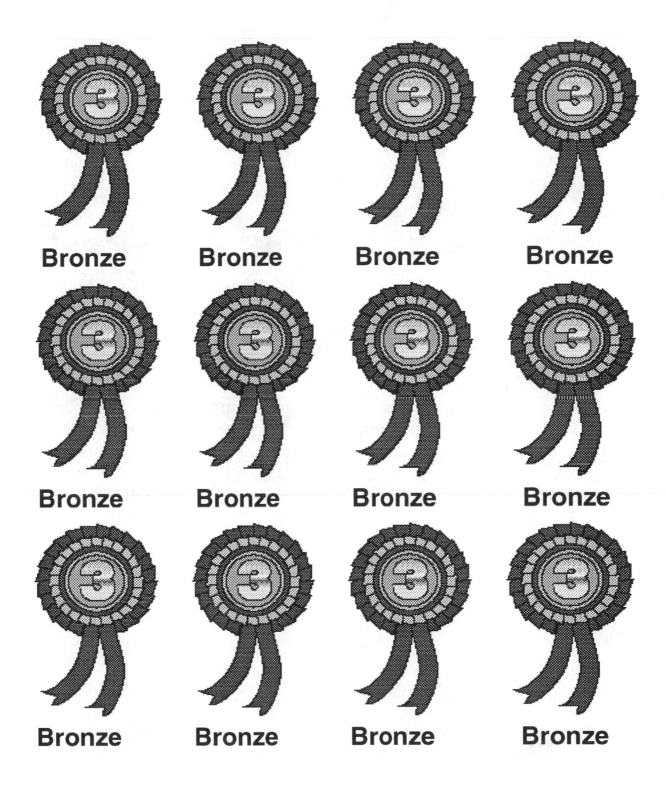

Bronze	Bronze	Bronze	Bronze
Bronze	Bronze	Bronze	Bronze
Bronze	Bronze	Bronze	Bronze

Our "Olympics" Stations

1. Potato Boxing

Equipment:
- 3 tablespoons
- 3 potatoes
- 1 folding chair (**Note:** A station sign is taped to the back of the chair. The chair is also useful in case a volunteer parent needs to sit down.)

Formation: The students line up at the folding chair. Three players stand in a designated area, holding a potato on a tablespoon.

Ya missed me!

Action: On a signal each player attempts to knock the potatoes (knockdown) from the spoons of the other players, while at the same time trying to keep his own potato from being knocked off. Players may jump, dodge, twist, and turn in the action, but may not use their hands to protect or hold their potato in place. When a player loses his potato from the spoon, he is eliminated from the game.

Awards:
- First player out   = Bronze Medal
- Second player out   = Silver Medal
- Remaining player   = Gold Medal

2. Arm Wrestling

Equipment:
- 1 tumbling mat
- 1 folding chair

Formation: Students line up at the folding chair. Two students lie on the mat, facing one another. The two students will arm wrestle each other.

Action: On the command, "Go," each child attempts to force the back of his opponent's hand to the mat. Whoever succeeds becomes the winner. Students may choose to repeat with the left hand for a second chance.

Awards:
- Winner = Gold Medal
- Non-winner = Silver Medal

3. Beanbag Balance

Equipment:
- 3 beanbags
- 1 cone
- 1 folding chair

Formation: Students line up at the folding chair. Students balance the beanbags on their heads (begin with one and progress up to three). A cone stands approximately 10 yards away from the chair.

Action: Students attempt to walk around the cone and back while balancing one beanbag on their heads. If successful, repeat with two beanbags, etc. The students are not allowed to touch the beanbags with their hands at any time.

Awards:
- 1 beanbag = Bronze Medal
- 2 beanbags = Silver Medal
- 3 beanbags = Gold Medal

4. Battleship

Equipment:
- 3 tumbling mats
- 3 small cones
- 9 nerf balls
- 6 scooters
- 1 folding chair

Formation: Build the three battleships by placing a folded tumbling mat on two scooters (it should make a large skateboard). Place a cone on each battleship. Two students are assigned to a battleship.

Action: The partners work together as follows. One person sits on the battleship and the other person pushes. On the command "Go," the battleships are pushed around the area. The people on the battleships throw the nerf balls at the other ships, trying to knock the cones off the ships. The pushers must drive the battleships around to gather nerf balls. The rider may not leave the battleship. The cone cannot be adjusted if hit. The battleship team is out if the cone falls off the ship.

Awards:
- First battleship out = Bronze Medal
- Second battleship out = Silver Medal
- Remaining team = Gold Medal

5. Back to Back Race

Equipment:
- 1 folding chair
- 1 cone

Formation: Three pairs of students race at one time. Pairs should be lined up with the folding chair. The cone is placed approximately 15-20 yards away.

Action: Students sit back-to-back on the ground with elbows interlocked. On the signal "Go," each pushes against the other's back as they attempt to straighten their legs and rise simultaneously to a standing position. The pair (with elbows still interlocked) run around the cone and back.

Awards:
- 1st place = Gold Medal
- 2nd place = Silver Medal
- 3rd place = Bronze Medal

6.   Javelin Throw

Equipment:
- 1 folding chair
- 3 air bananas (or other suitable objects)
- 3 cones

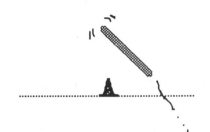

Formation: Students line up at the folding chair. The first cone should be about 5 yards away. The second cone is 5 yards behind the first. The third cone is 5 yards behind the second. These distances can be adjusted as needed.

Action: Students stand three steps behind the starting line (the folding chair). They may take steps up to the starting line and then throw the air banana as far as possible without stepping past the line.

K-2 Awards:
- Attempt   = Bronze Medal
- 1st cone   = Silver Medal
- 2nd cone   = Gold Medal

3-5 Awards:
- 1st cone   = Bronze Medal
- 2nd cone   = Silver Medal
- 3rd cone   = Gold Medal

7.   **Clean House**

Equipment: • 1 folding chair
 • 3 long jump ropes
 • Yarn balls

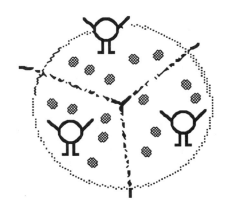

Formation: Students line up at folding chair. Jump ropes are laid out on the ground with handles touching in the center and ropes stretched outward to evenly divide a pretend circle into three sections. An even number of yarn balls are placed in each third of the circle. One student stands in each section.

Action: On the signal "Go," the students begin tossing the yarn balls into the other students' sections, trying to "clean house." The adult times for 30-60 seconds (depending on the length of the line) and says "Stop." The one with the cleanest house wins.

Awards: • Fewest yarn balls   = Gold Medal
 • In between   = Silver Medal
 • Most yarn balls   = Bronze Medal

8.   **Mystery Feely Box**

Equipment: • 1 folding chair
 • 1 box of stuff
 • 1 list of stuff

Formation: Students line up at the folding chair.

Action: With eyes closed, the student places his hand in the box and tries to identify objects in the box.

Awards:		
• 5 correct guesses	= Gold Medal	
• 3 correct guesses	= Silver Medal	
• 1 correct guess	= Bronze Medal	

9. **Penny Toss**

Equipment:
- 1 folding chair
- Muffin tin
- 5 pennies

Formation: Students line up at the folding chair. Place the muffin tin about 6 feet in front of the chair.

Action: Each student stands next to the chair and attempts to toss the five pennies into the muffin tin.

Awards:		
• 2 or more pennies	= Gold Medal	
• 1 penny	= Silver Medal	
• Participates	= Bronze Medal	

10. **Scoops**

Equipment:

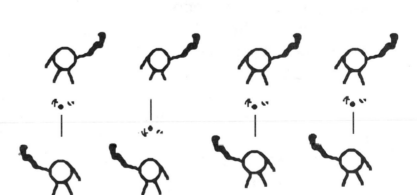

- 1 folding chair

- 8 scoops

- 4 whiffle balls

Formation: Students line up at the folding chair. Pairs of students play this game standing about 12 feet apart (vary the distance for age).

Action: Two students play catch with the scoops and a ball.

Awards:
- Gold = 10 consecutive catches
- Silver = 6 consecutive catches
- Bronze = At least 3 consecutive catches

(You may have to vary the standards after a while if these are too easy or too hard.)

11. Egg Toss

Equipment:
- 1 folding chair
- Many plastic eggs filled with water
- 2 large buckets of water

Formation: Students line up at the folding chair. Three pairs of students compete against each other at the same time.

Action: Give one water-filled egg to each pair of students. They stand about 10 feet away from each other as shown (the distance can be modified for different ages). Make sure that the eggs are all on the same side.

Say "Toss." The students gently toss their eggs to their partners. If an egg breaks open, that pair is done. Have successful pairs take a step backwards and repeat. Keep repeating as necessary.

Awards:
- Bronze = first pair out
- Silver = next pair out
- Gold = remaining pair

12. Target Throw

Equipment:
- 1 folding chair
- 2 tables
- 6 nerf balls
- 6 bowling pins

Formation: Students line up at the folding chair. Place a table about 10 feet from the chair. Stand the bowling pins on the table in a 1-2-3 formation.

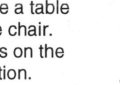

Action: Student stands at the folding chair and gets to throw 3 nerf balls to knock the pins over.

Awards:
- Gold = Knocked all of the pins off the table.
- Silver = Knocked all of the pins down.
- Bronze = Knocked at least 1 pin down

13. Clothespin Drop

Equipment:
- 1 folding chair
- 1 jar
- 5 clothespins

Formation: The students line up at the folding chair. Place the jar on the ground in back of the chair.

Action: The student kneels on the folding chair and attempts to drop the clothespins into the jar. He must hold his hand up even with his nose before dropping the clothespins.

Awards:
- Gold = 4 clothespins in jar
- Silver = 2 clothespins in jar
- Bronze = Tried

14. Hula Hoop Marathon

Equipment:
- 1 folding chair
- 12 hula hoops

Formation: Students line up at the folding chair. Three or more students may participate at one time.

Action: Each student receives two hula hoops. On the signal, "Go," the students swing two hula hoops around their waists at one time for as long as possible. A student is done when both hula hoops have hit the ground.

Awards:
- Gold = last one left with 1 or 2 hula hoops
- Silver = next to the last one left
- Bronze = the rest that participated

(You may choose to have the younger children use just one hula hoop.)

15. Frisbee Toss

Equipment:
- 1 folding chair
- 6 hula hoops
- 5 frisbees

Formation: Students line up at the folding chair. Scatter hula hoops on the ground beyond the chair.

Action: Each student stands at the folding chair and throws five frisbees (one at a time) attempting to land them into the hula hoops.

Awards:
- Gold = 3 frisbees in hoops
- Silver = 1 frisbee in a hoop
- Bronze = Participated

16. Jumbo Jets

Equipment:
- 1 folding chair
- Pack of paper
- 2 hula hoops
- Garbage bag

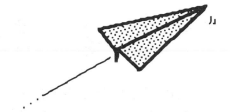

Formation: Students line up at the folding chair. Place one hula hoop 6 feet from the chair and the other hula hoop 4 feet past the first one.

Action: Each student receives one piece of paper and designs his own paper airplane. When the airplane is completed, the student stands by the folding chair and tries to fly the plane so that it lands in-side into a hula hoop. The student may save the airplane or place it in the garbage sack.

Awards:
- Gold = plane lands inside the far hoop
- Silver = plane lands inside the near hoop
- Bronze = plane flies

17. Bowling

Equipment:
- 1 folding chair
- 12 bowling pins
- 2 bowling balls

Formation: The students line up at the folding chair. Set up two bowling lanes with six pins each.

Action: The students stand next to the folding chair. Each student receives two rolls of the ball to knock down as many pins as possible. Have the students reset the pins after their turns.

Awards:

- Gold = all pins knocked down on first roll (strike)
- Silver = all pins knocked down with 2 rolls (spare)
- Bronze = tried

18. Goofy Golfing

Equipment:
- 1 folding chair
- 3 animal coffee cans
- 3 hockey sticks
- 3 whiffle balls

Formation: The students line up at the folding chair. Place the three coffee cans out in front of the folding chair (to use as three different stations). Three students may play at a time.

Action: The students begin at the folding chair and try to hit the whiffle ball into the can with the hockey sticks. Keep trying until it goes in.

Awards:
- Gold = took 3 putts to get it in
- Silver = took 4 putts to get it in
- Bronze = took 5 or more to get it in

19. Birdie in a Basket

Equipment:
- 1 folding chair
- 6 badminton birdies
- milk crate

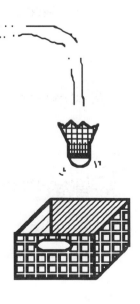

Formation: The students line up at the folding chair. Place the milk crate 6 feet from the chair.

Action: The student stands next to the folding chair and tosses six birdies into the crate.

Awards:
- Gold = 3 birdies in the crate
- Silver = 2 birdies in the crate
- Bronze = Tried

20. Basketball Shoot

Equipment:
- 1 folding chair
- 1 basketball score clock
- 3 mini basketballs
- 1 extension cord

Formation: The students line up at the folding chair. The basketball 30-second time clock will already be set up outside a classroom. The 30-second clock will be plugged into the extension cord and run into the classroom.

Action: A student shoots mini basketballs at the hoop until time is up. You may choose to have younger children just take three shots instead of using the 30-second timer. The timer starts with the first basket.

K-2 Awards:
- Gold = 8 points
- Silver = 4 points
- Bronze = 2 points

3-5 Awards:
- Gold = 20 points
- Silver = 12 points
- Bronze = 4 points

21. 3-Way Tug of War

Equipment:
- 1 folding chair
- 1 sturdy rope tied in a loop
- 3 jump ropes

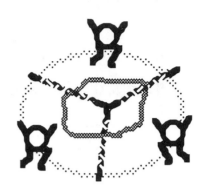

Formation: The students line up at the folding chair. Lay the jump ropes on the ground with the handles touching in the middle and the ropes stretched out away from the middle to divide the ground into three sections. Place the cone on top of the handles in the center. Put the looped rope on the ground so that the cone is in the center. Place one student in each section. Have them pick up the rope and hold it.

Action: On the signal "Go," all three students begin pulling backwards from the center. Each student tries to pull the other two students out of their areas.

Awards:
- Gold = last person to stay in his area
- Silver = next to the last person
- Bronze = first person to leave his area

22. Soccer Shoot

Equipment:
- 1 folding chair
- 2 cones
- 1 broken hula hoop
- 3 soccer balls

Formation: The students line up at the folding chair. Put the ends of the broken hula hoop into the cones to make a goal. Place the goal about 10 feet from the folding chair.

Action: A student stands even with the chair. He gets three chances to kick a ball through the soccer goal.

Awards:
- Gold = Goal on first kick
- Silver = Goal on second kick
- Bronze = Tried

Teamwork Field Day

"Teamwork" Field Day

Background: Our "Teamwork" Field Day is designed to take place in one afternoon (approximately 2 hours) for a total of 600 students at one time. The **20 activity stations** are set up carnival style on our two playfields and the blacktop area. This is an outstanding field day format where students in all grade levels are interacting in spirited teamwork activities.

Teamwork Cards: The students are given a Teamwork Card to be colored in class. Each "warm fuzzy" cartoon guy needs to be colored a different color of the rainbow (one red, one orange, one yellow, one green, one blue, and one purple).

Grade-by-Grade Nametags: Each student wears a different colored name tag to identify his grade level (K=purple, 1st=blue, 2nd=green, 3rd=yellow, 4th=orange, and 5th=red).

Teamwork Required: All of the games require teamwork of **two or more students**. When a student plays a partner game, a sticker is put on the appropriate "warm fuzzy" cartoon guy based on his partner's nametag color/grade level. This encourages students to play the games with someone from each grade level. When a student plays a team game, a sticker is put on the appropriate letter of Teamwork. The station descriptions will indicate when this occurs. The circled C and J are for the cookies and juice station.

Format: We conduct our field day in the afternoon. The "Teamwork" Field Day begins with an all-school assembly on the blacktop. Our teachers demonstrate some of the partner and team games. We finish the assembly with the entire school singing a song called, "Rainbow Planet," by Jim Valley. Classroom teachers had a copy of the tape and words in their classrooms for a month prior to field day. We also used the song quite often during our physical education classes throughout the year.

The games are spread out around the playground and the students are encouraged to try as many games as possible. There is no set rotation. The games are run by parent volunteers. The teachers walk around, play the games, talk with students, and of course, supervise.

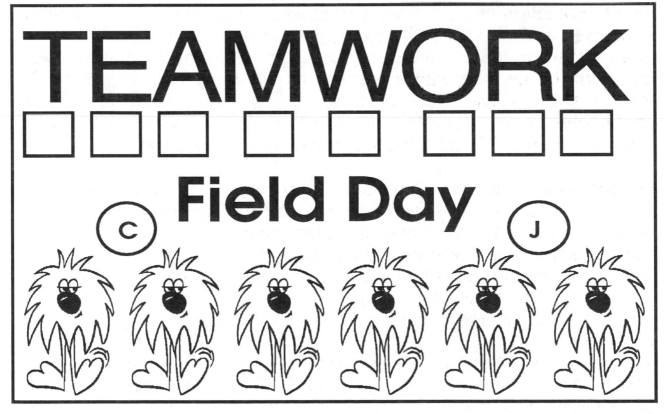

Our "Teamwork" Stations

1. **Junk Jog**

   Equipment:
   - 1 folding chair with directions
   - 4 Nerf balls
   - 1 Catchit ball
   - 2 hula hoops
   - 1 orange cone
   - Colored peel and stick stickers

   Set Up: Place all of the play equipment on the ground next to the folding chair. Set the cone on the ground approximately 20 steps away from the folding chair.

   Play: Partners must begin by holding hands (only one hand each). Together they must carry all equipment around the cone and back in one trip. If something drops, they must stop and pick it up.
   After completion, the parent volunteer places a sticker on the "warm fuzzy" cartoon character that matches each partner's nametag color.

2. **Wheelbarrow Course**

   Equipment:
   - 1 folding chair with directions
   - 6 orange cones
   - Colored peel and stick stickers

   Set Up: Place the cones in a straight line for a zig-zag course (about 4 steps apart).

Play: One person holds the feet of his partner in a wheelbarrow position. The wheelbarrow zig-zags around the cones to the other end, where the partners trade positions and return around the cones to the folding chair. After completion, put a sticker on the "warm fuzzy" cartoon that matches each partner's nametag color.

3. **Hoop Shoot**

   Equipment:
   - 1 folding chair with directions
   - 3 towels
   - 3 Nerf balls
   - Colored peel and stick stickers

   Set Up: This game requires being set up at a basketball hoop.

   Play: Partners each hold one end of a towel. Place a Nerf ball on the towel. Together they try to toss the ball off of the towel and through the basketball hoop. Let them try as many times as they want (unless there is a long line). After completion, put a sticker on the "warm fuzzy" cartoon that matches each partner's nametag color.

4. **Bowling**

   Equipment:
   - 1 folding chair with directions
   - 10 plastic bowling pins
   - 1 Nerf ball
   - Colored peel and stick stickers

   Set Up: Find a place next to a brick wall (the building). Set the 10 pins as in real bowling.

Play: One partner bowls the first roll and the other partner bowls the second roll. Together they pick up the pins for the next people. After completion, put a sticker on the "warm-fuzzy" cartoon that matches each partner's nametag color.

5.   **Scoops**

Equipment:
- 1 folding chair with directions
- 8 yellow plastic scoops
- 4 whiffle balls
- Colored peel and stick stickers

Set-up: Find an open space where the students will be able to play catch without interfering with other games.

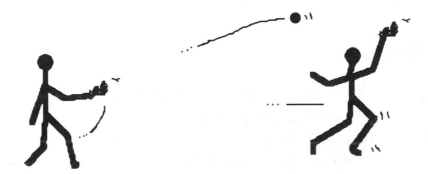

Play: Let pairs of students play catch using the scoops and a ball. They may want to start close together and step back each time they have a successful catch or they may just want to play catch. After completion, put a sticker on the "warm-fuzzy" cartoon that matches each partner's nametag color.

6.   Back to Back Course

   Equipment: • 1 folding chair with directions
                   • 7 orange cones (tall ones)
                   • 3 jump ropes
                   • Colored peel and stick stickers

Set-up: Place the ends of a jump rope into the tops of two cones to make a hurdle. For this station you will need three hurdles. Place the hurdles about 10 feet apart. Place the seventh cone out a little further.

Play: The partners sit on the ground back to back and lock elbows. Together they stand up, then walk together over the hurdles, around the cone, and back over the hurdles again. They must stay attached throughout the event. After completion, put a sticker on the "warm-fuzzy" cartoon that matches each partner's nametag color.

7.   Musical Chairs

   Equipment: • 1 folding chair with directions
                   • Portable tape player
                   • Music tape
                   • Small colored cones
                   • Colored peel and stick stickers

Set-up: Use small colored cones to outline a large circle (approximately 10 feet in diameter). Place the tape player on the folding chair.

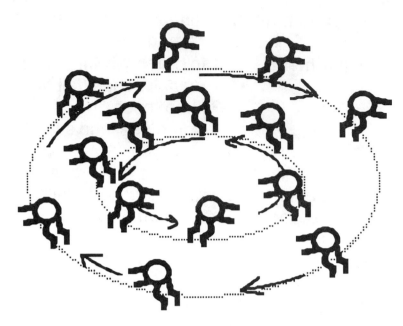

Play: This game takes at least three sets of pairs. The more the better. Play the music. One partner walks clockwise in the center of the circle while the other partner walks counterclockwise outside the circle. When the music stops, the partner in the outside circle goes down on one knee to form a chair. The inside circle partner must sit on his partner's knee. The last pair seated is out. Repeat until there is just one

pair left. Be sure that players are sitting down carefully. This game can get wild if not closely supervised!

After completion, put a sticker on the "warm-fuzzy" cartoon that matches each partner's nametag color.

8. **Bodyominos**

Equipment:
- 1 folding chair with directions
- Giant flash cards with designs
- Colored peel and stick stickers

Set-Up: Choose an area on the grass with plenty of room for this activity station.

Play: Each student needs a partner. Show the pairs of students one of the cards (easier designs for little kids, harder designs for older kids, etc.). The pair must lay down on the grass and make the same design using their bodies together.

After completion, put a sticker on the "warm-fuzzy" cartoon that matches each partner's nametag color.

9. **Goofy Golf**

Equipment:
- 1 folding chair with directions
- Coffee cans
- 3 hockey sticks
- 3 plastic whiffle balls
- Colored peel and stick stickers

Set-Up: Choose a grassy area. Set the three cans up in a miniature golf course. Keep the sticks and the balls near the folding chair.

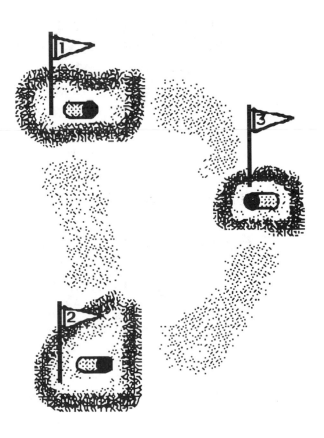

Play: Partners go through the golf course together using one stick and one ball. One partner hits the ball with the hockey stick in the direction of the first can. The other partner takes the next putt. They continue to take turns until they have completed the course.

After completion, put a sticker on the "warm-fuzzy" cartoon that matches each partner's nametag color.

10. Jump Rope Twins

Equipment:
- 1 folding chair with directions
- 6 single jump ropes
- Colored peel and stick stickers

Set-Up: Find a spot to set up on the blacktop.

Play: Each pair is given one jump rope. The pair must work together so that both partners are jumping the rope at the same time.

After completion, put a sticker on the "warm-fuzzy" cartoon that matches each partner's nametag color.

11. Balloon Squeeze

Equipment:
- 1 folding chair with directions
- Blown up balloons
- Extra balloons to blow up
- 1 orange cone
- Colored peel and stick stickers

Set-Up: Choose a spot on the grassy field. Place the cone about 15 giant steps away from the folding chair (use your own judgment). Keep the bag of balloons near the folding chair.

Play: This game is played with a partner. Partners face each other and place a blown up balloon between their foreheads. Together they must walk around the cone and back without dropping the balloon. If the balloon drops they must replace it before making any forward progress.

After completion, put a sticker on the "warm-fuzzy" cartoon that matches each partner's nametag color.

12. **Hula Hoop Pass**

    Equipment:
    - 1 folding chair with directions
    - 16 hula hoops
    - Colored peel and stick stickers

    Set-Up: Find a spot on the grass with plenty of room. Keep the hula hoops in one stack.

    Play: This is a team game that needs at least six players. The students stand side by side holding hands in a line. The student on the end picks up a hula hoop and climbs through it passing it on to the next person. The idea is to pass all 16 hula hoops to the other end as quickly as possible. Students may not let go of hands and must climb through all of the hula hoops!

    After completion, place a sticker under the letter "T" in the word "Teamwork."

13. **Tug of War**

    Equipment:
    - 1 folding chair with directions
    - 1 large tug of war rope
    - 3 orange cones
    - 1 colored jersey
    - Colored peel and stick stickers

    Set-Up: Choose a spot on the grass. Tie the jersey around the center of the rope to mark the middle. Place a cone to mark the middle of the playing area. Match the middle of the rope to the middle cone. Place the other two cones about four steps from the middle cone.

Play: This is a regular tug of war game. Use 3-4 players to hold each end of the rope. On the signal, "Go," they work

together to pull the jersey part of the rope past their own cone. Remind the students not to slide their hands on the rope or they might end up with rope burns. After completion, place a sticker under the letter "E" in the word "Teamwork."

14. Battleship

Equipment:

- 1 folding chair with directions
- 3 gray folded mats
- 6 wooden scooters
- 3 cones
- 9 Nerf soccer balls
- Chalk
- Colored peel and stick stickers

Set-Up: Choose a fairly flat spot on the blacktop. Draw the boundaries using chalk. Place a folded mat on two scooters to make the three battleships. Place one cone on the front of each battleship. Scatter the balls.

Play: There are three players per battleship. One player sits on the battleship. He is the ball thrower. The other two teammates push the battleship and collect balls to give to the thrower. On the signal, "Go," the throwers try to knock the cones off the other battleships by throwing the balls. The throwers may protect their own cone, but may not hold on to it. A team is out when their cone is knocked off the battleship.

After completion, place a sticker under the letter "A" in the word "Teamwork."

15. Soccer

Equipment:
- 1 folding chair with directions
- 1 soccer ball
- 2 broken hula hoops
- 4 orange cones
- 6 inner tube bands
- Colored peel and stick stickers

Set-Up: Find a large grassy area. Make two goals using the broken hula hoops and the cones (place the ends of a hula hoop in orange cones). Set the goals about 20 steps apart.

Play: This game needs at least two players for each team. The team members pair up and tie the inner tube bands around their inside ankles (similar to a 3-legged race position). Team pairs must play soccer connected to partners. It helps if they put their arms around each other's shoulders for balance. There should be enough bands so that teams can have at least three pairs each playing soccer at the same time.

After completion, place a sticker under the letter "M" in the word "Teamwork."

16. **Bodybands**

Equipment:
- 1 folding chair with directions
- Colorful, elastic stretch bands (Dyna Bands)
- Giant flashcards with designs
- Colored peel and stick stickers

Set-Up: Find a grassy area. Leave the bands and the cards on the folding chair.

Play: Groups of three or more students hold one band at waist height. The parent volunteer chooses a card for them based on the number of students in the group (easy designs for smaller groups, harder designs for larger groups, etc.). The group attempts to make the same design with the band.

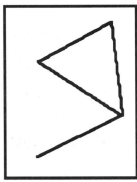

Hint: The students may need to hold the band with more than just their hands!

After completion, place a sticker under the letter "W" in the word "Teamwork."

17. **Volleyball**

Equipment:
- 1 folding chair with directions
- Volleyball net and standards
- Beachball
- Colored peel and stick stickers

Set-Up: Use volleyball standards and a net to set up an outdoor volleyball court.

Play: Let the students play volleyball using the beachball. The parent volunteer determines the number of students and the length of the game depending on the number of students waiting in line to play.

After completion, place a sticker under the letter "O" in the word "Teamwork."

18. **Team Jog**

 Equipment:
 • 1 folding chair with directions
 • 3 jump ropes
 • 1 orange cone
 • Colored peel and stick stickers

 Set-Up: Place the cone at least 50 yards away from the folding chair.

 Play: Teams of four or more students hold one jump rope and jog together around the cone and back (the rope keeps them together).

 After completion, place a sticker under the letter "R" in the word "Teamwork."

19. **Karaoke**

 Equipment:
 • 1 folding chair with directions
 • Stereo system with microphone
 • Karaoke player and tapes

Set-Up: Use the same set-up that was used for the opening ceremony.

Play: Student(s) choose which song to sing. Play the tape. Sing the song. Rewind the tape. Next person.....

After completion, place a sticker under the letter "K" in the word "Teamwork."

I've gotta be me!

20. Snacks

Equipment:
- 1 folding chair with directions
- Table(s)
- Cookies
- Juice
- Cups
- Colored marker
- Garbage cans
- Masking tape

Set-Up: If possible, choose a shady spot for this station. Put the cookies and the juice on a table with the garbage cans nearby.

Cross off the circle with a "C" (cookie) and cross off the circle with a "J" (juice).

21. Awards Stand

Equipment:
- 1 folding chair with directions
- Scotch tape
- Gold seals
- Certificates
- Table and chairs
- Folding mat

Set-Up: Set up the table on the blacktop near the karaoke station.

Play: Students will come to this station with completed cards. If they have a sticker in each TEAM-WORK square, they receive a certificate. The parent volunteers write the students' names and the date on their certificates for them. If they have a sticker on each color "warm fuzzy" cartoon character, they also receive a gold seal to put on their certificate.

TEAMWORK

Award

Presented to: _____

Physical Education Teacher   Principal   Date

Great Activities Publishing Company

Circle of Games Field Day

"Circle of Games" Field Day

Background: This is a unique field day format with endless possibilities! Each class will compete against another class in a variety of fun games and relays.

How We Do It: Here's how it works. You'll need enough stations to accommodate two classes per station. For example, if you have 20 classes, then you will need 10 stations. **Two classes are assigned to a station**. These two classes compete against each other. Sometimes the whole class participates and sometimes just 8-12 students per class participate at a time.

Once the activity is completed, one class rotates clockwise and the other class goes counter-clockwise to the next station.

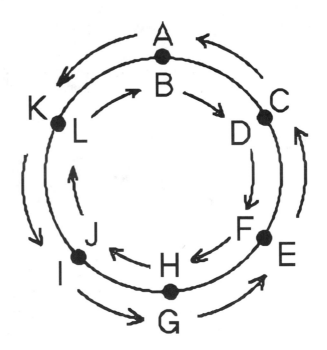

For example, after Classroom A and Classroom B finish their station, they will move to the next station as shown.

The classes on the outside circle go to their right and the classes on the inside circle go to their right. This will bring together two new classes!

Parent Volunteers: Each of the activity stations is supervised by parent volunteers. Some of your stations can be designated as a water break or snack station.

Our Stations

1. The Little 500

Equipment:
- 2 tricycles
- 2 Big Wheels
- 2 scooters
- Cones for race track boundaries

Activity: Everyone in each class participates. If one class is smaller than the other, assign students to go twice. Students will use the three vehicles to race around the designed race track. The first player uses the tricycle, the next player uses the Big Wheel, and the third player uses the scooter. This continues until the race is over.

2. Rescue 911

Equipment:
- 4 cones

Activity: Ten students per class will participate in this activity at a time. The children will stand in a line with a cone 15 yards in front of each line. The first child will run down, around the cone and return to take the second child's hand and repeat the process. Both of the children will round the cone holding hands and return for the third child. Continue this process until the whole team completes the race as a unit. Repeat the relay with the remaining students.

3.   **Carry Me Back Home**

   Equipment: •   4 cones

   Activity: The entire class
   participates in this activity.
   Each class needs to travel to
   the finish line from the starting point in the correct carrying position. Classes may
   travel in groups of five to
   seven. The correct carrying
   position is as follows: Students stand side by side and

   grasp each others forearms.   This forms bridges where other stu-
   dents will sit while holding on to the shoulders of the "bridge makers."
   You may switch the "bridge makers" during the event as the contest
   continues. No time outs. The first class to get all of the students
   across the finish line will be declared the winner.

4.   **Is He Dizzy?**

   Equipment: •   2 cones
             •   2 Zoogle sticks (or whiffle ball bats)
             •   2 mats

   Activity: This activity involves the whole class. Ten students are
   chosen to be obstacles in this event. Five students squat one in front
   of the other, approximately 10 feet from the starting cone. Twenty
   feet from the last squatter, five students will stand in a straddle position - one in front of the other. Ten feet from the last straddler is a
   mat with a Zoogle stick or plastic bat.

On the signal to begin, the first person at the starting line leap frogs over each squatter, scrambles under each individual straddler, runs to the mat and grabs the Zoogle stick. One end of the stick is placed on the ground. The student places his forehead on the top end of the stick and runs around in a circle three times. The student then runs back, avoiding obstacles, and tags the next person. The first group to finish wins. Some students may go twice to even the class numbers or the teacher may participate.

5. **Tubular Knot**

    Equipment: • 2 tires
                    • 4 cones

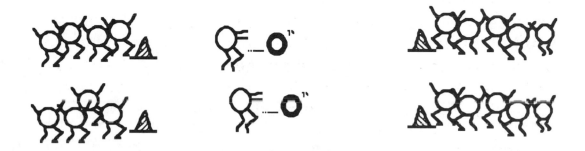

    Activity: This activity will use 10 students per class at a time. Each group of students will divide in half, with five standing at the starting line and the other five standing 50 yards away from the starting line. On the signal to begin, the first person will roll the tire down to the teammate at the opposite side of the field. This person then rolls it back. The first group done wins. Repeat the relay with the remaining students.

6. **Chariots of Tire**

    Equipment: • 2 tires
                    • 10 short ropes
                    • 4 cones

    Activity: Tie the five ropes to each tire. The classes need to be split into five or six teams of five players. To even out the teams, one student may go twice.

One student will sit on the tire and hold one of the short ropes, while the others grasp the end of one of the other ropes which are also tied to the tire. On the signal to begin, the students pull the tire and rider around the cone and back. When they get back to the starting line, the second team goes. Repeat the relay until all of the students have participated. Have the teachers straighten the ropes for each team of their relay.

7. Water Sponge Toss

Equipment:
- Sponges
- Buckets filled with water
- Cones

Activity: Set up the cones to mark the boundary for each class to stay behind. One class at a time gets their sponges and throws them high into the air across to the other class. Students get 1 point for each sponge they catch. After all of the students in one class have thrown the sponges, the other class has a turn. Repeat as often as time permits.

8. Buddy Walkers

Equipment:
- 4 cones
- 2 sets of Buddy Walkers

Activity: Have the students in each class pair up. Partners will stand behind the starting line and wait for the signal to begin. When the race starts, the first set of partners will move together down and around the far cone and back. The first class to finish is the winner.

9.   **Tug of War**

  Equipment: • Tug of war rope
              • 2 cones
              • 1 whistle

Activity: This activity will use 10 students per class at a time.   Each class comes to the rope and stands next to the rope in their desired positions. Nobody is to touch the rope until instructed to do so. On the signal "Go!," both lines start pulling. The object of the game is to pull the opponents past your cone. When the whistle sounds, all participants must stop pulling. Remember, ropes can burn you - let go!!!
Repeat the activity with the remaining students.

10.   **3-Legged Creature Feature**

  Equipment: • Bicycle inner tube loops
              • Cones for marking the race area

Activity: This activity will use five sets of partners from each class at a time. Each set of partners will attach the bicycle inner tube loop around the inside legs. On the signal to begin, the first pair will move as quickly as possible around the cone and back. They will then tag the next pair as the relay continues. Repeat the relay with the remaining students.

"A⁺ for Effort"

Field Day Award

**The Bearer of this Certificate was
An Active Participant in Our
Field Day!**

Physical Education Teacher   *Principal*

Great Activities Publishing Company

Battle Creek Field Day Stations

Battle Creek Field Day Stations

Background: Described below are several field day stations that have been created by the Battle Creek Public School Physical Education Staff. We had a fantastic time creating all of these ideas. Please feel free to include them in your next field day!

1. Wet Sponge Throw

Equipment:
- Buckets filled with water
- Sponges
- Targets on the wall or fence

Activity: Students will reach into a bucket filled with water and grab a sponge. They will attempt to throw the water-filled sponge at the target on the wall or fence. If they hit the target, they get 5 points for their team. Missing the target gets no points. Each student will throw one sponge and retrieve it for the next person on the team to take a turn.

2. America's Cup

Equipment:
- Foil pans
- Ping pong balls
- 1 long table
- Water in foil pans
- Cones to mark the starting line

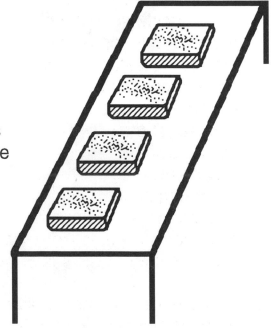

Activity: On the signal to begin, the first person in each team runs to the pan filled with water. This person places a ping pong ball at one end of the pan and sails his "Yacht" across the pan by blowing on it. Upon completing the "course," the player picks up the ball and returns to the starting line. This continues until all players have completed a turn.

226

3.   **Alphabet Relay**

    Equipment: • 2 sets of alphabet cards
                   • Cones to mark the starting line

    Activity: Place a set of 26 alphabet cards about 30 feet from each team. The first player runs to the alphabet cards that are scattered on the ground, picks up one and returns to the start. The next person does the same. This continues until all of the cards are picked up and placed in alphabetical order back at the starting line. The cards do not have to be picked up in alphabetical order, but the cards must be placed in order at the starting line.

    ⌐A⌐ ⌐B⌐ ⌐C⌐ ⌐D⌐
    ⌐T⌐ ⌐Y⌐

4.   **Rat Tag**

    Equipment: • 1 jump rope for every student
                   • Cones to designate the boundaries

    Activity: Students all tuck a rope at their waist (in the back) so that it hangs and touches the ground. If a student has a one-piece outfit on, they may place it in a pocket. The students find a position inside the playing area. On the signal to begin, each tries to step on the tail of the other player. If the tail is stepped on, it must be left on the ground. The students may not use their hands to grab another player's tail.

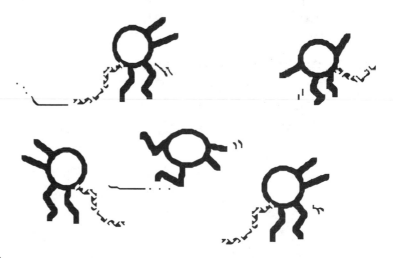

All students continue to play even though their rope has been taken. Stop play when one or two students still have their rope. Have the students replace the ropes and start another game as time permits.

5.   **Towel Toss**

Equipment:

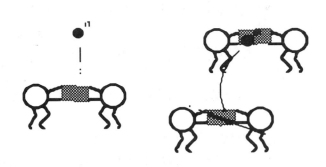

- Beach towels
- Light-weight balls

Activity: Students will be in groups of two. They will work together to toss the ball up in the air and catch it using only the beach towel. Students are to see how many times they can do this in succession. They can try to throw it very high or throw it fancy ways . . . as long as they are having fun.

6.   **Noodle Relay**

Equipment: • Swimming pool foam noodles
 • Cones for marking the race area

Activity: In pairs, the students will hold the pool noodle between their legs and race to the cones and back. This can be done as often as time allows, changing positions on the noodle, changing teams, or having three at a time on the noodle.

7.   **Tootsie Roll Relay**

Equipment: • 4 pairs of women's-sized garden gloves
 • Bowls of Tootsie Roll midgets
 • Table
 • Small garbage can for wrappers

Activity: Students start at the line. On the signal to begin, the students put on the garden gloves. They then run to the table and pick up a Tootsie Roll and place it in their mouth after unwrapping it. They chew the tootsie roll and then return to the next person and give them the gloves. This continues until all students have had a chance.

8. Jumping Station

Equipment:

- Short jump ropes

- Long jump ropes

- Jump bands

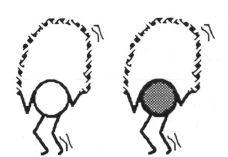

Activity: Students select a piece of equipment and jump. They can trade ropes or jump bands whenever they choose.

Certificate of Achievement

We hereby recognize

_____

in honor of a great Field Day!

_____   _____   _____
PE Teacher   _Principal_   _Date_

Great Activities Publishing Company

Certificate
of Merit

The Bearer of this Certificate was an Outstanding Participant in Our Field Day!

_____
Date

_____   _____
Principal   P.E. Teacher

Great Activities Publishing Company

Wacky Olympics Field Day

"Wacky Olympics" Stations

Background: Welcome to the Wacky Olympics Field Day. In this field day, the **students select a partner** and are allowed to visit each station at their own pace and comfort. This way the students do not need to worry about missing an activity that they really want to do.

The following 25 activities can be adapted to your own field day ideas. Please feel free to modify or change them to suit your situation. Have fun!

1. String Diving

Equipment:
- 8 - 10 yo-yos
- 4 diabolos

Activity: The students have fun working with the yo-yos and diabolos. If it becomes too busy, set a time limit in order for everyone to get a chance to work with the equipment.

2. Water Spray Golf

Equipment:
- 4 spray bottles
- Buckets of water to refill bottles
- 4 cones
- Ping pong balls
- Golf tees

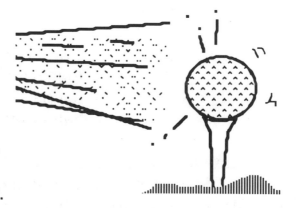

Activity: The students stand behind the line (the cones) and try to knock the ping pong balls off the golf tee that is placed 1 yard away.

The students squirt water from the spray bottle to do this. Once the ball is knocked off, that student will place the ball back on the tee for the next player.

✗3.   Gumnastics

    Equipment: • Bubble gum - one piece per student
                   • Trash can to collect the gum

    Activity: The students receive a piece of bubble gum. They may choose to blow bubbles on their own or choose "team blowing" and everyone blows on command. The gum must be spit out before leaving the activity station.

✗4.   Canoe Hook It?

    Equipment:

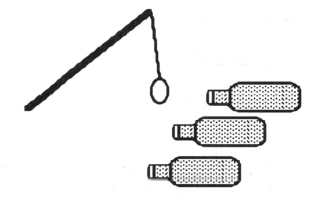

         • 8-10 one-liter bottles
         • 2 "fishing poles" with a ring
           on the end
         • 2 tables

    Activity: Two students have a "fishing pole" with a ring on the end. The liter bottles are lying on their sides on the tables. With the ring, they try to hook the neck of the bottle and stand up as many of them as possible in one minute.

5.   Field Hockey

    Equipment: • 2 gym hockey sticks
                   • 2 tennis balls
                   • 4 cones
                   • 2 cardboard boxes

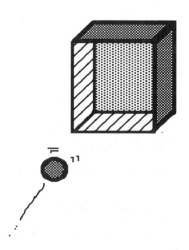

    Activity: Two students at a time are given a gym hockey stick and a tennis ball. They travel down the field striking the tennis ball and shoot at one of the cardboard goals.

✳ 6.   Opening Ceremonies

Equipment:
- 2 Hawaiian-print polo shirts
- 2 sunglasses
- 2 Sports Illustrated magazines
- 2 water bottles
- 2 tickets
- 4 cones

Activity: In this activity, the students pretend they are going to the opening ceremonies of the Olympics. Using a relay format, the first person in each team will put on the shirt and sunglasses, carry the water bottle, magazine and tickets and run around the cone and back.

✳ 7.   Double's Tennis

Equipment:
- 1 paddleball racquet for each pair
- 1 tennis ball for each pair
- 4 cones

Activity: At this station, two students race against two other students. On the signal to begin, the partner will carry the tennis ball on the racquet to the designated cone and back without dropping the ball. If the ball is dropped, the student will retrieve it and start from that spot.

8.   Tour de France

Equipment:
- 2 hula hoops
- 4 cones

Activity: On the signal to begin, each student will roll his "bike tire" (hula hoop) to the cone, around it, and back. The next person will continue the race by rolling the "bike tire" to the cone, around it, and back.

9. 50-Yard Dash

Equipment:
- 4 cones
- String for the finish line

Activity: On the signal to begin, the students will race 50 yards to the finish line. Have two students hold a long piece of string for the finish line.

10. Baton Relay

Equipment:
- 1 baton per team
- Cones

Activity: Students will have a partner for this race. The partner will wait at the cone set 30-40 yards from the starting line. The first partner will start with the baton. On the signal to begin, the first partner runs down and passes off the baton to his partner who runs down, around the starting cone and back to the first partner, where he passes the baton back to the first partner. The first partner runs back to complete the race.

The first partner runs to the cone.

The second partner runs around the cone and back to the first partner.

The first partner runs back to complete the race.

11. Hurdles *steeple chase*

Equipment:
- Various size boxes
- 1 cone used as an end line for each relay team

Activity: Mark off three to four lanes using the boxes lined up with a cone at the end of each lane. The students will, on the signal to begin, hurdle over the boxes, run to the cone, around it, and back, hurdling the boxes on the return trip also.

12. Mini-Javelin Throw

Equipment:
- Different colored toothpicks
- Bed sheets

Activity: One-by-one, the students will throw a toothpick for distance onto the sheets which are spread out on the ground. The student with the longest throw is the winner.

13. Shot Putt

Equipment:
- Softballs
- 4 cones used as the standing line

Activity: Everyone with a softball will stand behind the line. On the signal to begin, all students will throw their softballs from a stationary position. The older grades can take two or three hops before the throwing line, but may not cross it. Students will retrieve their own softball. Please make sure that the area is well marked off for safety and that the students wait to retrieve the softballs until all have finished.

14. Discus

Equipment:
- Frisbees
- 4 cones

Activity: For safety reasons, the students will stand in one spot for the throw. If you feel comfortable, you may allow the students to take a 360° turn before tossing the frisbee. Students retrieve their own frisbees once everyone has thrown.

15. **B-Ball**

    Equipment:
    • Basketballs
    • Basketball goals
    • Cones

    Activity: For the older students, 4th - 6th grades, have a free throw contest or let them play a basketball game. The younger ages may have a dribbling relay contest around the cones and back to the next person in line.

16. **Synchronized Sponges**

    Equipment:
    • Sponges
    • Buckets with water

    Activity: Students will be placed into partners. Each person will stand facing his partner who will be 2 feet in front of him. Each student has a wet sponge. On the signal to begin, both partners will toss their sponge. If each partner catches the sponge, they both take one step backwards. If a sponge is dropped, that team is finished. Continue until there are only 2 or 3 teams left.

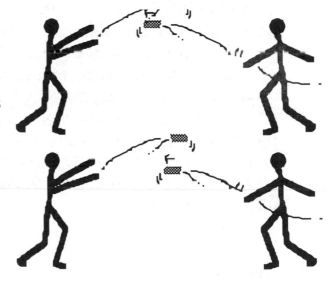

17. **Bubbles**

    Equipment: • Bubbles and wands

    Activity: Each student will make fabulous bubbles with the wand and soap mixture. Who can make the biggest bubble?

18. Running Long Jump

Equipment:
- Long jump sand pit
- Mark a white line for the take off point
- Measuring tape
- Rake for the sand pit

Activity: The students will run and jump into the sand pit as far as they can. Students can take two jumps.

19. Foosbowling

Equipment:

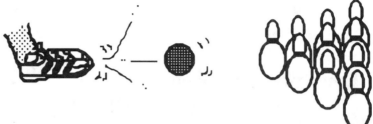

- 1 soccer ball
- Bowling pins

Activity: The students will kick the ball at the bowling pins, trying to knock them over. Keep score for each student. You will need someone resetting the pins after each kick; or, have each student retrieve the soccer ball and reset the pins after his turn.

20. Face Painting

Equipment: • Face paint materials

Activity: It may be advisable to have a parent helper who has some practice with face painting. You may want to ask some older students to help with the younger students.

21. Athlete's Village

Equipment:
- Sidewalk chalk
- Pavement/sidewalks

Activity: Students will draw and create an athletes' village with sidewalk chalk. Encourage them to draw different flags, sporting events, equipment and athletes at the Olympic Village.

22. The Jungle Gym

Equipment:
- Climbing ropes
- Floor mats under each rope
- Stopwatch

Activity: This takes place in the gym using the climbing ropes. The students may climb on the ropes. Those who wish to be timed, may do so.

*23. Let It Fly

Equipment:
- Surgical tubing tied in a loop
- Beanbags
- "Targets" that are different sizes

Activity: This activity takes place in the gym. The students sit on the floor and will use their legs and the surgical tubing to make a "sling-shot." The student places a beanbag on the tubing, lifts his feet to aim, and pulls the tubing back. Students will shoot three beanbags, trying to hit the targets. Targets should be at different distances to challenge all skill levels.

24. Drink Station

Equipment:
- Drinks
- Cups
- Ice
- Trash cans
- Table

Activity: Your Olympic athletes have had a busy day. Let them have a bit of a rest in the "Rest-Awhile" Cafe.

* bathroom station

Best Partner Award

In recognition for being such a great partner!

Thanks for making this Field Day the best ever!

Given By	*School*	*Date*

Great Activities Publishing Company

Field Day Sparklers

Field Day Sparklers

Background: At our school we have a series of activities that provide two full days of fun field day games. One day is for our first and second graders and the other day is for our third and fourth graders. The PTA provides a cook-out lunch for the students, plus some really great watermelon and ice cream for dessert.

Field Day Sparklers: Our kids have enjoyed these games, activities, and other suggestions that really make our field days sparkle with fun!

1. **Awesome Kickball (1st & 2nd Graders)**

    Equipment: • 2 bases or cones
    • 1 nerf or foam ball

    Activity: Divide the class into two teams. One team kicks first while the other team is in the field. The fielding team must stand behind the pitcher when the ball is pitched. When the ball is kicked, the kicker runs to first base.

    The kicker runs continuously back and forth from home to first base. One point is scored for each time the kicker touches first base or home. When the ball is fielded, all of the members on the fielding team line up behind the player with the ball. The ball is then passed to each other between the legs. The last person in line then yells "Field Day."

    This action "freezes" the kicker and he may not run anymore. If he is on a base, he is safe; if he is off a base, he is out. The kicker is also out if the ball is caught. If the ball is dropped or if a person does not pass it between his legs, the team must start passing the ball from the leader again.

The teams change sides when there are three outs or if everyone on the kicking team has had a turn.

2.   **Teacher Ball (3rd & 4th Graders)**

     Equipment: • 1 hula hoop - or a circle drawn on the ground
                        • 4 Bases
                        • 1 tennis racquet (bat)
                        • 1 tennis ball

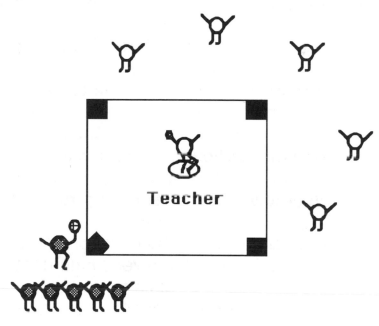

Activity: The game is played using a traditional diamond. Use the hula hoop to designate the pitcher's mound. The teacher acts as the pitcher. The students will have three jobs to do in this game:

• **Job #1:** The batter hits the tennis ball with the racquet and runs to first base. The batter advances to each base at his own risk.

• **Job #2:** The base runner advances when the ball is hit or, if stealing, on the release of the pitch by the teacher.

• **Job #3:** The fielder will retrieve the ball and run it, throw it, or relay it to the teacher who is standing in the hoop as quickly as possible. This includes balls that are caught in the air.

When the ball in is the teacher's hands, the base runners are frozen. They are safe if they are on a base; out if they are off base. A caught fly ball is also an out, and any runners on base may not advance. Switch sides after three outs, or once through the batting order.

3.   **Primary Scavenger Hunt (1st & 2nd Graders)**

     Equipment: • Paper bags
                         • Scavenger hunt list

Activity: Each group of 3-4 students is given a list of scavenger hunt items and a paper bag to collect the items. Please see the next page for a sample list.

4.   **Directional Scavenger Hunt (3rd & 4th Graders)**

     Equipment: • Directional scavenger hunt lists
                         • Directional signs or maps (optional)
                         • Assorted items (pennies, bags, etc.)

Activity: Each group of 3-4 students is given a list of directions. The students need to follow the directions in order. When finished, the group reports back to the Directional Scavenger Hunt station. Please see the next page for a sample list.

5.   **Exercise Scavenger Hunt (3rd & 4th Graders)**

     Equipment: • Paper bags
                         • Scavenger hunt list
                         • Mats for curl-ups/push-ups
                         • Pencils

Activity: Each group of 3-4 students is given a scavenger hunt list. Directions include:

1. Please read the directions carefully.
2. The items must be completed in order.
3. Team must agree on which way to go.
4. Don't come back until you have completed all of the items on the list.
5. No arguing or your team will be disqualified.

Primary Scavenger Hunt Items

Directions: Please collect as many of the items below as possible. You must travel as a group.

#1:	Three twigs	**#6:**	Two weeds
#2:	A small rock	**#7:**	A piece of paper
#3:	A leaf from the "big tree"	**#8:**	A clover leaf
#4:	A dandelion	**#9:**	A piece of hair
#5:	A piece of litter	**#10:**	Four different leaves

Directional Scavenger Hunt

Directions: Read the directions below and go as a group to collect the hidden items. Good luck!

1. Go to the softball backstop facing the gym. Pick up one bag. You are now facing EAST. You will need to remember this.

2. Turn SOUTH and go to the red hula hoop. Once at the hoop, find one tennis ball. Place the ball in your bag.

3. Turn to face WEST. Go to the nearest tree. Behind the tree is a chair. Pick up one penny from the chair. Put this in the bag.

4. Turn SOUTH and go to the soccer goal. Check the NORTH-EAST corner of the goal and take a popsicle stick. Put this in the bag.

5. Scatter your team to search for a piece of litter. Collect one piece per team member. Place it in the bag.

6. Return to the Directional Scavenger Hunt station. You are now finished!

Exercise Scavenger Hunt

Directions: Whenever possible, you must link arms throughout this scavenger hunt! It must be completed in order. Good luck!

Check-Off:

___ 1. Say "Field Day is awesome!" ten times.

___ 2. Perform 20 jumping jacks.

___ 3. Touch five trees.

___ 4. Collect three twigs.

___ 5. Touch three people wearing the color yellow.

___ 6. Say "Hi" to five Moms or Dads.

___ 7. Perform 10 curl-ups.

___ 8. Collect three fallen leaves.

___ 9. Count to 100 by 5's and then by 10's.

___ 10. Sing your favorite Barney song to your classroom Mom or Dad.

___ 11. Run as far as you can while screaming.

___ 12. Say the alphabet forwards and then backwards.

___ 13. Skip to the basketball court.

___ 14. Say "Thank you" to your teacher.

___ 15. Walk back to the Exercise Scavenger Hunt station.

6.   **Parent Volunteer Station Sheets**

   Background: While the majority of parent volunteers generally arrive on time, there are always several who arrive after the field day has started. We have developed "Station Sheets" to help give a brief explanation for our volunteers. A sample is given below:

Station #6: "Hanging Silly Face"

Equipment Needed:	None
Location:	Monkey Bars
Directions:	Two students hang on the bars facing each other. Both can make funny faces to try and get the other person to drop first.
Names of Parent Volunteers:	• Candy Richards (Justin Richards, 2nd grade) • Larry McDonald (Spencer McDonald, 5th grade)

---

7.   **Field Day Planning Sheets**

   Background: One of the most important aspects of planning a successful field day is making sure you have all of the equipment needed for each station. For this reason, we have developed a generic planning sheet for each of our stations. These sheets are very helpful as a way to "double check" to make sure everything is ready. Here's a sample blank planning sheet:

Planning Sheet

Field Day Game: _____

Equipment Needed:

* _____
* _____
* _____
* _____
* _____

Station Location: _____

Set-Up: _____
_____
_____
_____
_____

Directions: _____
_____
_____
_____
_____

8.   Wall of Fame

Background: During your field day, parents and students are able to nominate individuals to the Field Day "Wall of Fame." You'll need a table, "Wall of Fame" certificates, markers, and scotch tape. The certificates are filled out by the students, teachers, or parents and taped up for all to see. Here is a sample certificate:

Field Day Wall of Fame

I would like to commend

_____

for the following reason(s):

_____

_____

_____

Given By _____

Great Activities Publishing Company

Super Parent Volunteer Award

This certificate is given to:

_____

for making our Field Day so successful!

_____ _____ _____
Principal *Physical Education Teacher* *Date*

Great Activities Publishing Company

250

Friend of Physical Education Award

Thank you for your outstanding contributions during our Field Day!

_____   _____
Physical Education Teacher   *Date*

Great Activities Publishing Company

Contributors

We would like to thank the following physical education teachers for their contributions to this book.

Randy Furukawa (T.E.A.M. Field Day, page 5) teaches for the Kent School District in Kent, Washington. He has been teaching since 1981 and served on the writing committee that developed the new Washington State Health and Fitness Essential Learnings.

Clare Davich (Day at the Races Field Day, page 11; An Ocean of Fun Field Day, page 13; County Fair Field Day, page 25) teaches for Fort Wayne Community Schools in Fort Wayne, Indiana. She has taught physical education for over 15 years.

Nina Carter (Fun for All Field Day, page 33) teaches elementary physical education in Virginia. Her goal for her elementary students is for each of them to find personal "joy" through movement!

Jenny Aubel (American Plains Field Day, page 41) teaches for Loudoun County Public Schools, in Leesburg, Virginia. She has taught for over 15 years.

Amy Clark (Great Relay Field Day, page 49) teaches in Indianapolis, Indiana.

Jim Davis (Color Team Field Day, page 55) has taught for over 33 years. He lives in Woodstock, New York, and enjoys reading and playing tennis.

Pam Ihmels (Super Kids Field Day, page 63) teaches for Bismarck Public Schools in Bismarck, North Dakota. She is a former North Dakota Elementary Physical Education Teacher of the Year and has been teaching for over 20 years.

Connie Kapral (Fitness Festival Field Day, page 75) teaches for Glastonburg Public Schools in Connecticut. An elementary physical educator, she is also the Executive Director for Connecticut AHPERD.

Contributors

Maureen Kavanagh (School Pride Field Day, page 93) lives in Salem, Maine.

Sharon Kotovsky (Great Games Field Day, page 99) teaches for Fairfax County Schools in Fairfax, Virginia. She has been teaching elementary physical education since 1989.

Rip Marston (World Records Field Day, page 109) teaches at the University of Northern Iowa. He is the author of <u>The Great Activities' Parachute Book</u>!

Jim Ross (Think Tank Field Day, page 117; International Games Field Day, page 135) lives in Ridgewood, New Jersey. He is a former New Jersey Elementary Physical Education Teacher of the Year and has presented at numerous conferences across the country.

Krista Winn (BINGO Field Day, page 149; Fit, Healthy, and Ready to Learn Field Day, page 159; Livin' in the Country Field Day, page 169; Olympics Field Day, page 181; Teamwork Field Day, page 199) teaches for the Port Angeles School District in Port Angeles, Washington. She has been teaching for over 15 years.

Gwen Pribble (Circle of Games Field Day, page 217) is a former Indiana Elementary Physical Education Teacher of the Year and has been teaching for over 18 years.

Carrie Pennock (Battle Creek Field Day Stations, page 225) teaches for Battle Creek Public Schools, in Battle Creek, Michigan. She credits her fellow elementary physical education teachers for her success.

Kim Rampmeyer (Wacky Olympics Field Day, page 231) teaches in Anchorage, Alaska. She has been teaching for over 15 years.

Charlene Schneckenberger (Field Day Sparklers, page 240) teaches for the Lake Shore Central School District in New York. She has been teaching for over 12 years.

254